D1291295

Decision Support, Analytics, and Business Intelligence

Decision Support, Analytics, and Business Intelligence

Second Edition

Daniel J. Power
University of Northern Iowa

Decision Support, Analytics, and Business Intelligence, Second Edition
Copyright © Business Expert Press, 2013.
All rights reserved. No part of this publication may be reproduced, stored in a retrieval system, or transmitted in any form or by any means—electronic, mechanical, photocopy, recording, or any other except for brief quotations, not to exceed 400 words, without the prior permission of the publisher.

First published in 2009 by
Business Expert Press, LLC
222 East 46th Street, New York, NY 10017
www.businessexpertpress.com

ISBN-13: 978-1-60649-618-3 (paperback)

ISBN-13: 978-1-60649-619-0 (e-book)

DOI 10.4128/9781606496190

Business Expert Press Information Systems collection

Collection ISSN: 2156-6577 (print)
Collection ISSN: 2156-6593 (electronic)

Cover design by Jonathan Pennell
Interior design by Exeter Premedia Services Private Ltd.,
Chennai, India

First edition: 2009
Second edition: 2013

10 9 8 7 6 5 4 3 2 1

Printed in the United States of America.

Abstract

Competition is becoming more intense. Decision makers are encountering increasing complexity, rapid change and higher levels of risk. In many situations, the solution is more and better computerized decision support, especially analytics and business intelligence. Today managers need to learn about and understand computerized decision support. If a business is to succeed, managers must know much more about information technology solutions.

This introductory text is targeted to busy managers and MBA students who need to grasp the basics of computerized decision support, including: What is analytics? What is a decision support system? How can managers identify opportunities to create innovative computerized support? Overall this resource addresses 61 fundamental questions relevant to understanding the rapidly changing realm of computerized decision support.

In a short period of time, readers can "get up to speed" on decision support, analytics and business intelligence. The text then provides a quick reference to important recurring questions.

Keywords

analytics, business intelligence, decision support, decision support systems, decision making, knowledge management, computerized support, business applications, basic concepts, types of decision support, innovative DSS

Contents

Acknowledgments..ix

Introduction xi

Chapter 1   Modern Decision Support 1

Chapter 2   Decision Support Concepts 17

Chapter 3   Recognizing Types of Decision Support............31

Chapter 4   Business Intelligence and Data-Driven DSS.....53

Chapter 5   Predictive Analytics and Model-Driven
             Decision Support..75

Chapter 6   Decision Support Benefits and Trade-Offs 97

Chapter 7   Identifying Decision Support Opportunities.................113

Chapter 8   Looking Forward to Innovative Decision Support 127

Notes..137

Glossary 141

References and Bibliography..149

Index 157

List of Questions With Links to Answers 163

Acknowledgments

Many people over the years have contributed to the ideas and advice developed in the first and second editions of this book—my students, readers of my newsletter, faculty colleagues in the Association for Information Systems Special Interest Group on Decision Support, Knowledge and Data Management Systems (SIGDSS), friends in various software companies, and friends associated with the BeyeNETWORK™, a TechTarget company. My website DSSResources.com is a partner site of http://www.b-eye-network.com. Our sites provide "comprehensive resources for business intelligence and data warehousing professionals."

The actual production of this improved and expanded second edition is the result of the efforts of many people at Business Expert Press and affiliated organizations.

Last, and most importantly, I want to acknowledge the invaluable help and support of my wife Carol and my sons Alex, Ben, and Greg. You motivate me to do good work.

Many thanks to all of the people who helped make this revised and updated book titled Decision Support, Analytics and Business Intelligence a reality.

Introduction

We work in a period of significant economic and social change complicated by rapid technology advances in communications and computing. We have access to a vast storehouse of information on the Internet that often changes our perception of events and our understanding of our own lives and of products and services we create and use. The complexity, uncertainty, and turmoil of modern life has necessitated an expanded use of technology so we can stay connected with each other and to support our decision making. We live in an information rich, rapidly changing, highly competitive global marketplace of goods and ideas. In this environment, managers need to adopt information technology solutions that provide an edge in terms of better, faster, and more fact-based decisions.

Today managers must have extensive knowledge about information technology solutions and especially computerized decision support. Rapid technology change and innovation makes this task challenging, but managers have an obligation to shareholders to learn about and understand analytics, business intelligence, and decision support. This book is a knowledge resource targeted to busy managers and MBA students who want to learn the basics of decision support.

Managers should buy and read this primer on analytics, business intelligence, and decision support because it provides an overview of fundamental concepts related to computer support for decision making and answers to questions about using technology to support managers and operations decision makers in recurring and semistructured decision situations. Managers must continually adapt to competitive challenges and find ways to use technology to act faster, to act smarter, and to engage customers and stakeholders. Decision making is speeded up and the information available is sometimes almost overwhelming. No longer do we have large, uninterrupted blocks of time to contemplate and reflect, rather judgments are often hurried and information is incomplete. In this period of change and turmoil, technology not only causes information overload problems that managers encounter, but technology also provides tools to filter and manage information to provide more relevant and useful information to managers when they need it and want it to support their decision making. We have come to expect that information and communications technologies are solutions to problems.

Some topics covered in subsequent chapters include: What is business intelligence (BI)? What is a decision support system (DSS)? What is decision automation? What do managers need to know about computerized decision support? What are best practices for BI reports? What are the rules for building a successful model-driven DSS? What are potential benefits of decision support? How can managers identify opportunities to create innovative decision support? The goal in assembling this resource has been to address fundamental questions that are relevant to understanding computerized decision support.

In a few hours of reading and skimming, most managers can enhance their understanding of decision support, analytics, and business intelligence. Following familiarization with the content, this book then serves as a quick reference for answers to important recurring questions. Questions are arranged in a logical order with a mix of both general and more specialized questions of interest to managers and future managers. Decision support basics are fundamental definitions, facts, and principles about using information technologies to assist in decision-making processes.

Understanding the basics can help managers evaluate software vendor claims and can facilitate implementation of computerized decision support. In general, achieving the benefits of decision support capabilities advertised by a software vendor is a function of (a) the software purchased, (b) implementation activities, and (c) knowledge and training of technology staff and managers.

In the years ahead, we face a period of economic turmoil with many opportunities to use information technologies to improve decision making. It is easy for software vendors and system integrators to promise benefits from decision support, but often much harder to deliver them. DSS have been in use for many years, so it is likely that some readers have been involved with decision support, some may have taken relevant courses, and some have been on decision support project teams. Over the years, various experiences have convinced us that decision technology solutions can help make better decisions, and help organizations operate better and compete more effectively.

We want to make better decisions and find ways for our organizations to compete more effectively. Meeting these goals is only possible today if we use more and better computing and information technologies in novel ways to gather, process, and disseminate relevant information to decision makers in a timely manner. Computers, the global Internet, and wireless communications dominate the technology environment of twenty-first century businesses and organizations.

An organization's future is impacted by many internal and external factors and changes, but managers also initiate change and can build decision support capabilities that help meet real needs. There are many benefits of analytics, BI, and decision support, but informed users make the systems technologists build and implement better, and knowledgeable managers can help identify obsolete or poorly designed legacy systems. Managers with knowledge of decision support technologies can intelligently discuss potential applications and perceived needs with technology specialists. Knowledge about decision support concepts and practice is rapidly changing so this book is a progress report and not a final record made after a completed journey.

For over 35 years, my professional life has focused on using computers to support managerial decision making. During those years, my reading, interviews, consulting, and research projects using a variety of decision aiding technologies have led to my conclusions related to decision support. Decision support has been useful and companies and managers will realize even greater benefits from modern decision support, analytics, and business intelligence.

Since 1995, the World Wide Web has been a major communication mechanism for my ideas and research about decision support. Since May 2000, my newsletter, *DSS News*, has been providing managers and academic researchers current information and answers to important questions about topics on decision support. My Website called DSSResources.com is a premier source of articles, news, and case studies related to the field of computerized decision support. Much of the content that follows has appeared in *DSS News* or in articles for my Decision

Support Expert channel on the BeyeNETWORK™ (cf., http://www
.b-eye-network.com). The following material have been edited and
updated based on reader feedback, recent research, and technology
developments. Subsequent chapters provide my perspective about how
computers and information technology can assist managers in decision
making.

CHAPTER 1

Modern Decision Support

Managers must make decisions in an increasingly complex, rapidly changing, volatile, and ambiguous environment. This environmental turbulence increases risks for managers and organizations. To help reduce and manage risk now is an opportune time to implement more and better computerized decision support. Managers should implement or update systems to provide better business intelligence (BI), analytics, and other types of computerized decision support. This turbulent environment should motivate managers to evaluate computerized decision support projects. What has changed? Modern decision support is more useful and more sophisticated.

In the past 25 years, software vendors have regularly used new terms for capabilities associated with decision support. For some vendors, legacy terms such as *decision support system* (DSS) were rejected as too general, while for others legacy terms reminded potential customers of failed projects or unrealistic expectations. A new term such as *analytics* provided a new start for selling a decision support capability. Despite the changing terminology, managers continue to want and need computerized information systems to support their decision-making.

Decision support does not insure correct decisions. One hopes vendors have realized it is important to identify and better manage customer expectations. Decision support applications differ widely depending upon the purpose of the system and perceived need. Current technologies can support a wide range of decision-making tasks. Decision support consultants, designers, and researchers have learned much about using information technology (IT) solutions to support decision making and that knowledge can benefit managers and their organizations.

Prior research and experience supports two fundamental premises associated with computerized decision support. First, computers and IT can help people make important decisions. Second, computerized decision support assists and supports managers, and keeps them as part of the decision-making process. The overriding goal of computerized decision support developers is unchanged—*improve human decision-making effectiveness and efficiency with IT solutions.*

Many organizations have integrated computerized decision support into day-to-day operating activities and use systems for performance monitoring. Frequently, managers download and analyze sales data, create reports, and analyze and evaluate forecasting results. DSS can help managers perform tasks, such as allocating resources, comparing budget to actual results, drilling down in a database to analyze operating results, projecting revenues, and evaluating scenarios. Data warehouses can create a single version of the truth for advanced analytics and reporting. More managers are using business dashboards and scorecards to track operations and support decision-making.

Decision support research began in the 1960s and the concepts of decision support, decision support systems, and the acronym DSS remain understandable, intuitively descriptive, and even obvious in meaning. Related terms such as *analytics, BI,* and *knowledge management* are of more recent origin and are interpreted in different ways by vendors and consultants. Decision support is a broad concept that prescribes using computerized systems and other tools to assist in individual, group, and organization decision-making. One goal in this and succeeding chapters is to make some sense out of the decision support jargon.

The seven questions included in this chapter discuss the need for decision support, the technology skills and knowledge needed by managers, targeted users, a historical perspective on decision support, a theory of decision support, and adopting decision technologies. The final question identifies characteristics of modern decision support applications.

What Is the Need for Decision Support?

Today decision-making is more difficult: the need for decision-making speed has increased, overload of information is common, and there is more distortion of information. On the positive side, there is a greater emphasis on fact-based decision-making. A complex decision-making environment creates a need for computerized decision support. Research and case studies provide evidence that a well-designed and appropriate computerized DSS can encourage fact-based decisions, improve decision quality, and improve the efficiency and effectiveness of decision processes.

Most managers want more and better analyses and decision-relevant reports quickly. Managers do have many and increasing information needs. The goal of many DSS is to create and provide decision-relevant information. There is a pressing need to use technology to help make decisions better. Decision makers perform better with the right information at the right time. In general, computerized decision support can help transfer and organize knowledge. Effective decision support provides managers more independence to retrieve and analyze data and documents, as they need them.

From a different perspective, we need decision support because we have decision-making biases. Biases distort decisions. Reducing bias has been a secondary motivation for decision support, but it is an important one. Most managers accept that some people are biased when making decisions, but doubt a computerized solution will significantly reduce bias. Evidence shows information presentation and information availability influence and bias a decision maker's thinking both positively and negatively. Evidence shows system designers can reduce the negative bias. Also, evidence shows decision makers "anchor" on the initial information they receive and that influences how they interpret subsequent information. In addition, decision makers tend to place the greatest attention on more recent information and either ignore or forget historical information.[1] Good decision support software can reduce these and other biases.

Managerial requests for more and better information, today's fast paced, technology-oriented decision environments, and significant decision-maker limitations create the need for more and better computerized decision support. Managers should strive to provide computerized decision support when two conditions associated with a decision situation are met: (a) good information is likely to improve the quality of a decision, and (b) potential users recognize a need for and want to use computerized support in that situation.

Introducing more and better decision support in an organization does create changes and challenges for managers. For example, using a smart phone with decision support applications or a tablet PC connected to the Internet and corporate databases requires new skills and new knowledge of managers.

What DSS Skills and Knowledge Do Managers Need?

Technology skills quickly become obsolete. Concepts and theoretical knowledge have a much longer "half-life." Managers need to master the what, when, who, and why of computerized decision support. Managers need less knowledge about the how-to of computerized decision support, analytics, and BI systems. The concept of decision support has broadened over the past 50 years to encompass a wide variety of information technologies that support decision-making. The basic philosophy of decision support is that technology and software positively impact decision-making. Managers must know much more about IT solutions than when they began their careers.

Analytics, BI, and DSS use sophisticated information hardware and software technologies, and therefore, managers need computing and software knowledge to understand such systems. In addition, there is an increasing need for managers to provide input to hardware and software choices. At a minimum, in today's business environment, a manager needs to be able to operate the software environment of personal computing devices (e.g., a workstation, a portable computer, and a smart phone).

Our hardware and software environment is rapidly changing (i.e., new versions of Microsoft Office, new Google products, new hardware devices, and new intracompany web-based applications are introduced). In addition, managers often need to master software products relevant to the job. In some situations, it may be necessary to develop small-scale budgeting or cost-estimating applications in Excel or a product such as Crystal Reports. There is a growing need for "end user" development of small-scale DSS and preparation of special decision support and analytic studies.

Networks and enterprise-wide systems are expanding globally. Because managers and knowledge workers are the primary users of enterprise-wide DSS, managers must understand the possibilities and be involved in designing the systems. Managers need to develop the skills and knowledge to think about IT solutions, including defining a problem, formulating a solution, and implementing a solution.

Managers need to understand the benefits, costs, and risks of building a specific IT decision support capability. Decision support, analytics, and BI systems can solve problems and create new problems. Managers need broad knowledge of technology to help them make informed decision support implementation choices.

Computing and IT knowledge needs and skills are constantly evolving. We all need to learn continuously about new concepts and new skills. Some new decision support requirements build on previously learned materials; others force us to change our thinking dramatically.

Who Uses Computerized Decision Support?

Many people use computerized decision support for work and in recent years to aid in personal decision-making. Identifying the targeted or intended users for computerized decision support helps to differentiate the specific system. Knowing who does or will use a capability provides useful information about how the content and design of the application might or should differ. Let us review examples of job titles and occupations of targeted users for decision support, BI, and analytic systems.

In 1978, Keen and Scott Morton described six diverse systems and targeted user groups, including: (1) a DSS to help investment managers with a stock portfolio, (2) a DSS used by the president of a small manufacturing company to evaluate an acquisition prospect, (3) an interactive DSS used by product planners for capacity planning, (4) a model-driven DSS used by a brand marketing manager for making marketing allocations, (5) the geodata analysis and display system (GADS) used to redesign police beats, and (6) a DSS to explore and define alternative school district boundaries.

By 1996, Holsapple and Whinston identified many management users of decision support applications. For example, the management staff of the distribution department at Monsanto used a DSS for ship-scheduling decisions; a DSS helped managers with vehicle fleet-planning decisions; cargo planners used a DSS for scheduling ship unloading in

Rotterdam; plant supervisors at Dairyman's Cooperative used a PC-based DSS to optimize daily production planning; maintenance planners at American Airlines used a decision support application; and analysts and executives in the US Coast Guard used a document-driven DSS to help make procurement decisions.

Turban and Aronson also identified DSS used by staff for special studies. Staff at Group Health Cooperative used a data warehouse and statistical analysis tool to generate periodic reports and for monitoring key performance indicators, and staff at Siemens Solar Industries constructed a simulation model DSS of a "cleanroom" to explore alternative design options.

DSSResources.com has 52 decision support case studies that identify users, including managers, staff, customers, the general public, and workers in business, government, and not-for-profit organizations. Job titles of users include engineers, loan officers, salesmen, fire department commanders, examiners in the Pennsylvania Department of Labor and Industry, business and financial analysts, and emergency management professionals.

A web search identifies even more uses and users. For example, some medical doctors are using a web-based clinical DSS. DSS are used by judges, lawyers and mediators, farmers, and agricultural policy makers.

The US Marine Corps needed an application that allowed Marine Command staff to import, manipulate, and analyze terrain data relative to their operations. Road maintenance supervisors evaluated a maintenance decision support system during the winter of 2003 in Central Iowa. DSS are used for air traffic monitoring. Also, a DSS is used by staff to facilitate manpower planning for the US Marines. Military analysts use a financial data mart at the Military Sealift Command at the Navy Yard in Washington, DC. TIAA-CREF portfolio managers use a DSS for more than 160 billion US dollars of daily equity investment.

Fico.com cites many uses of predictive analytics by companies. The company's website claims "Predictive analytics is widely used to solve real-world problems in business, government, economics and even science—from meteorology to genetics." Managers and staff implement and use analytics and especially predictive analytics in credit scoring, underwriting, collecting past due accounts, increasing customer retention and up-selling, and fraud detection.

So who uses computerized decision support including analytics and BI systems? Managers, knowledge workers, and staff specialists in a wide variety of professions, occupations, industries, and disciplines. Decision support users include internal and external stakeholders of an organization. Ultimately, anyone who makes decisions and has access to a computer is a potential user of a computer-based decision aiding application.

What Is the History of Computerized Decision Support?

Some knowledge of the history of computerized decision support should help managers understand decision support and make better adoption decisions. This brief review of the evolution of decision support technology primarily touches on decision support innovations and successful projects (Figure 1.1). More details about decision support history are available at DSSResources.com.[2]

First Generation Decision Support

We can trace the origins of computerized decision support to 1951 and the Lyons Tea Shops business use of the LEO I (Lyons Electronic Office I) digital computer. LEO handled accounts and logistics. Software factored in the weather forecast to help determine the goods carried by "fresh produce" delivery vans to Lyons' United Kingdom shops.[3] Lyons innovated, but the new DSS was not sufficient to help managers adapt to changing customer needs.

On election day November 4, 1952, a computer application was used to predict the US Presidential voting results from exit interviews, but news reporters were skeptical of the prediction and did not use it. A few years later, work started on the Semi-Automatic Ground Environment (SAGE), a control system for tracking aircraft used by North American Aerospace Defense Command.

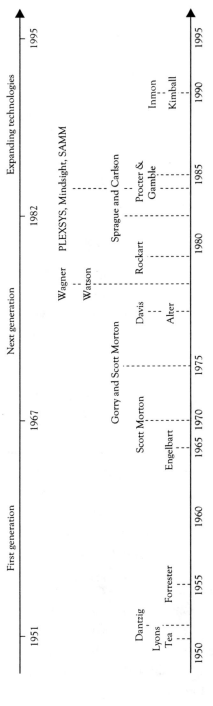

Figure 1.1. Decision support history time line.

The name SAGE, a wise mentor, indicated the decision support nature of the system. SAGE was a high cost, innovative real-time control, communication, and management information system (MIS).[4] The technology was quickly obsolete, but continued to function until the early 1980s.

The pioneering work of George Dantzig, Douglas Engelbart, and Jay Forrester established the feasibility of building a wide range of computerized decision support applications. In 1952, Dantzig, a research mathematician at the Rand Corporation, implemented linear programming on an experimental computer to solve a variety of analytical problems. In the mid-1960s, Engelbart and colleagues developed the first groupware system, called NLS (oNLine System). NLS had on-screen video teleconferencing and was a forerunner to group DSS. Forrester was involved in building the SAGE data-driven system. In addition, Forrester started the System Dynamics Group that built complex computerized, quantitative models for decision support at the Massachusetts Institute of Technology Sloan School.

Prior to about 1965, it was very expensive to build large-scale information systems. From 1965 onward, the new mainframe technology like the IBM System 360 and timesharing technology made it practical and cost-effective to develop MIS in large companies. MIS focused on providing managers with structured, periodic reports derived from accounting and transaction systems.[5] Technology developments stimulated decision support innovation and adoption.

Moving to the Next Generation

In the late 1960s, a new type of information system became practical, so-called model-oriented DSS or management decision systems. For his Harvard Business School doctoral research, Michael Scott Morton devised and studied a computerized management decision system. He studied how computers and analytical models could help managers make a key decision. Scott Morton conducted an experiment where marketing and production managers used a management decision system to coordinate production planning for laundry equipment. The decision system ran on a 21-inch cathode ray tube monitor with a light pen connected using a 2400 bits per second modem to a pair of UNIVAC 494 computer systems.[6] The computer support improved decision-making and planning.

In 1971, Gorry and Scott Morton argued that MIS primarily focused on structured decisions and suggested that the information systems for semi-structured and unstructured decisions should be termed as DSS.[7] The article initiated an academic subfield.

By the late 1970s, researchers were discussing both practice and theory issues related to DSS, and companies were implementing a variety of systems. In 1979, John Rockart published an article in the Harvard Business Review[8] that led to the development of executive information systems (EISs). In 1980, Steven Alter published a framework for categorizing DSS based on studying 58 DSS. He identified both data-oriented and model-oriented DSS.[9]

Ralph Sprague and Eric Carlson's book, *Building Effective Decision Support Systems,*[10] explained in detail a DSS architecture framework: database, model base, network, and dialog generator. In addition, they provided a practical, understandable overview of how organizations could and should build DSS. By 1982, many researchers considered DSS as an established class of information systems.

In the early 1980s, financial planning and modeling systems became especially popular decision support tools. The software idea was to create a "language" that would "allow executives to build models without intermediaries."[11] Analytical models gained acceptance in business decision-making.

By 1982, managers and researchers recognized that DSS could support decision makers at any level in an organization. DSS could support operations, financial management, management control and strategic decision-making. Technology and conceptual developments had expanded the scope, purpose, and targeted users for computerized decision support.

Generation 3: Expanding Decision Support Technologies

The scope and capabilities of computing technology expanded tremendously with the advent of personal computers. Spreadsheets made analysis of data and model building easier and faster. Researchers developed software to support group decision-making using local networks.[12] In 1985, Procter & Gamble built a DSS that linked sales information and retail scanner data. BI was embryonic as the decade changed, analysts were advancing a set of concepts and methods to improve business decision-making by using fact-based support systems. Companies were implementing briefing books, report and query tools, and EIS.[13]

In the early 1990s, Bill Inmon and Ralph Kimball actively promoted using relational database technologies to build DSS. Kimball was known as "The Doctor of DSS" and he founded Red Brick Systems. Inmon became known as the "father of the data warehouse" and founded Pine Cone Systems. From Inmon's perspective, a DSS involved "data used in a free form fashion to support managerial decisions."[14] The DSS environment of the 1990s contained only archival, time variant data. Both data warehousing and On-Line Analytical Processing (OLAP) technologies improved data-driven DSS.[15]

A major technology shift had occurred from mainframe and time-sharing DSS to client/server-based DSS at about this time. Vendors introduced desktop, personal computer–based OLAP tools. Database vendors recognized that decision support was different from online transaction processing and "started implementing real OLAP capabilities into their databases."[16] By 1995, large-scale data warehousing, a convergence of technologies and systems, and the possibilities for distributed DSS created by the World Wide Web stimulated innovation and created a renewed interest in computerized decision support and BI.

By 2000 possibilities for real-time decision support became more realistic. In 2012, developments in analytics, operational, and mobile BI continue to stimulate decision support innovation in organizations. Computer support for decision makers continues to expand and improve.

What Is the Theory of Computerized Decision Support?

Past practice and experience often guide computerized decision support development more than theory and general principles. Some developers have concluded each decision situation is different so no theory is possible. Some academics argue that we have conducted insufficient research to develop theories. For these spurious reasons, a theory of decision support has received limited discussion in the literature.

Nobel Laureate Economist Herbert Simon's writings provide a starting point for a theory of decision support. From his classic book, *Administrative Behavior,*[17] are derived three propositions:

> *Proposition 1*: If information stored in computers is accessible when needed for making a decision, it can increase human rationality.
>
> *Proposition 2*: Specialization of decision-making functions is largely dependent upon developing adequate channels of communication to and from decision centers.
>
> *Proposition 3*: When a particular item of knowledge is needed repeatedly in decision-making, an organization can anticipate this need and, by providing the individual with this knowledge prior to decision-making, can extend his or her area of rationality. Providing this knowledge is particularly important when there are time limits on decisions.

From Simon's article[18] on "Applying Information Technology to Organization Design" are three additional propositions:

> *Proposition 4*: In a postindustrial society, the central problem is not how to organize to produce efficiently, but how to organize to make decisions—that is, to process information. Improving efficiency will always remain as an important consideration.
>
> *Proposition 5*: From the information processing point of view, division of labor means factoring in the total system of decisions that need to be made into relatively independent subsystems, each one of which can be designed with only minimal concern for its interactions with the others.
>
> *Proposition 6*: The key to the successful design of information systems lies in matching the technology to the limits of the attention of users. In general, an additional component, person, or machine,

for an information-processing system will improve the system's performance when it:

1. has a small output in comparison with its input, so that it conserves attention instead of making additional demands on attention.
2. incorporates effective indexes of both passive and active kinds. Active indexes automatically select and filter information.
3. incorporates analytic and synthetic models that are capable of solving problems, evaluating solutions, and making decisions.

In summary, computerized decision support is potentially desirable and useful when there is a high likelihood of providing relevant, high-quality information to decision makers when they need it and want it.

What Influences Adoption of Decision Support?

Change and innovation continue to be related to computerized decision support. Some managers seem quick to purchase new technologies and try out new capabilities, others are slower to adopt an innovation. Adopting a new technology is the first step in building a new capability and gaining technology acceptance in an organization. Managers can adopt an innovation, but intended users may not accept the new technology. So why are some managers quick to adopt and others delay? Leaders and laggards are common among individuals and organizations in the adoption of technology. In the late 1950s, sociology researchers[19] proposed a technology adoption lifecycle model. Moore in his 1991 book *Crossing the Chasm*[20] proposed a variation of the lifecycle that identified a significant gap in time from when early adopters and more pragmatic managers buy technology. This gap is caused by the perceived disruption from the innovation.

Decision support technologies are often disruptive innovations. Also, some decision support innovations are quickly obsolete or "faddish." Some decision support applications are purchased and adopted, but quickly become dated or revised. Also, underused and poorly accepted software known as "shelfware" was bought and now sits on shelves in IT departments.

Buying or building a new decision support capability often is a significant decision. The new system may be a one-time purchase or an ongoing commitment of resources. Some general reasons why one company is often an early adopter of significant decision support innovation and another is often slow can be identified. Reasons include the availability of resources, risk propensity, knowledge of the technology, the culture, and senior management characteristics. The interaction of these factors is complex and that hinders a researcher or consultant trying to understand a particular company's situation.

Some more detailed reasons for slow adoption of innovative technologies are (1) mistrust between IT and business executives, (2) lack of data quality and too many data sources, (3) delayed infrastructure projects, (4) IT staff are poorly trained, and (5) new technologies are confusing and poorly understood. This list[21] of reasons suggests changes managers could make to encourage faster adoption of new technologies.

Adoption of decision support technologies should be a pragmatic, rational decision. Practical considerations should be the most important factor when managers adopt decision support technologies for their organizations. In some situations, organizations have benefited from early adoption of technology, but examples of waste and negative disruptions are also common. In general, managers should cautiously adopt a potentially disruptive decision support technology.

What Is Typical of Modern Decision Support?

Modern decision support started to evolve in about 1995 with the specification of HTML, expansion of the World Wide Web in society, and the introduction of handheld computing. Web 2.0 technologies, mobile integrated communication and computing devices, and improved software development tools have revolutionized decision support user interfaces. Additionally, company decision support data stores are growing in size and contain varied and extensive "big data." The fourth generation of computerized decision support is maturing.

We need to recognize that analytical systems often have multiple capabilities. Attributes of contemporary analytical and decision support systems typically include the following:

1. Access capabilities from any location at anytime.
2. Access very large historical data sets almost instantaneously.
3. Collaborate with multiple, remote users in real-time using rich media.
4. Receive real-time structured and unstructured data when needed.
5. View data and results visually with excellent graphs and charts.

Change is accelerating. Where is the current leading edge and what technologies are on the horizon that can be exploited to build more advanced decision support? Grid computing and parallelism seem particularly interesting. Both speech generation and recognition can be exploited; and stereographic displays and wearable computing technologies are improving.

Modern BI and DSS have more functionality than systems built prior to the widespread use of the Internet and World Wide Web. Managers are choosing to implement more decision automation with business rules and more sophisticated knowledge-driven decision support. Current systems are changing the mix of computing and decision-making skills needed by managers in organizations. There is a shortage of managers and analysts with the expertise to conduct analyses and use decision support capabilities.[22] Managers are realizing that better computerized decision support is crucial for competing in a global business environment.

Summary

Decision support and BI systems serve varied purposes and targeted users and are implemented with a variety of technologies. Analysis and interpretation of data from computerized sources is becoming a very important skill for managers. With current technologies, computerized applications can and do support a wide range of decision-making tasks.

Contemporary decision-making environments create a need for more, and better, computerized decision support.

A general understanding of decision support history provides a context for understanding modern decision support. The first generation systems were on mainframe computers, but the SAGE defense system provided sophisticated real-time decision support. By the 1980s, decision support technologies broadened the possibilities for computerized decision support to include collaboration and BI. Since approximately 1995, computer support for decision makers has significantly expanded and improved.

Nobel Laureate Herbert Simon's ideas provide a theoretical rationale for building computerized DSS and using analytics. Computerized decision support and analytics can expand the rationality of decision makers. Managers should adopt decision support capabilities when it is likely that significant benefits will be realized. Modern decision support assists decision makers and helps them make better decisions by exploiting new technologies and expanding capabilities. Modern decision support helps managers.

CHAPTER 2

Decision Support Concepts

For more than 30 years, companies have implemented decision support applications. Software and systems have changed and vendors have renamed and repurposed decision support applications to catch the attention of managers. Sometimes software vendor terminology is focused on the narrow purpose of the software; sometimes the focus is on the underlying technology; and sometimes the focus is on targeted users. For example, business activity monitoring has a narrow purpose focus. Data warehouse uses an analogy to a physical warehouse with a focus on the database technology. Executive Information Systems referred to a decision support application for a targeted user group.

Recently, primarily because of technological developments such as smart phones, managers have become more enthusiastic about implementing innovative decision support. This is a positive development, but both managers and technology staff need to examine their expectations for decision support to increase the chances of creating useful systems.

Computer-based decision support can provide managers with analytical capabilities and timely information that improve decision making. In pursuing this goal of improving decision making, vendors have built computerized systems to help individual decision makers and decision teams. Some systems provide structured information directly to managers. Other systems help managers and staff specialists analyze situations using various types of models. Some systems store knowledge and make it available to managers. Some systems support decision making by small and large groups. Companies even develop systems to support the decision making of their customers and suppliers.

This chapter reviews important decision support concepts and associated acronyms such as DSS, EIS, BI, BAM, BPM, and KM. The goal is to examine the purposes, technologies, and targeted users of these decision support capabilities. Understanding key terms helps us explain what is possible and what is desirable in supporting decision making.

What Is a Decision Support System?

DSSResources.com defines a decision support system (DSS) as:

> an interactive computer-based system or subsystem intended to help decision makers use communications technologies, data, documents, knowledge, and/or models to identify and solve problems, complete decision process tasks, and make decisions. Decision support system is a general term for any computer application that enhances a person or group's ability to make decisions. In general, decision support systems are a class of computerized information system that supports decision-making activities.[1]

Decision support system is a metacategory, as fruit is a metacategory for apples and oranges. Both decision support and DSS are broad, general terms that are intuitively understandable to members of an organization. Technologists and managers need to avoid overusing technical terms and information technology jargon with colleagues and staff.

DSS is a broad, inclusive term for more specialized systems built with technologies such as data warehouses, OLAP, desktop databases with query tools, document management systems, financial models, optimization models, knowledge management (KM) tools, expert systems, and groupware. Decision support describes the overriding purpose of many information systems.

In 1982, Sprague and Carlson stated that "DSS comprise a class of information system that draws on transaction processing systems and interacts with the other parts of the overall information system to support the decision-making activities of managers and other knowledge workers in organizations."[2] Some vendors, such as Information Builders, use this broad definition.

An online glossary at IBM Developer Works defined the term *decision support system* as "one of a number of older synonyms for applications and data used to support decision-making and business management processes, now broadly called business intelligence systems."[3]

The term *decision support system* refers to many specific systems and it is important to recognize how each differs or is similar. Traditionally, researchers have discussed building DSS in terms of four major components: (a) the user interface; (b) the database; (c) the models and analytical tools; and (d) the DSS architecture and network.[4] Evaluating these components helps to identify similarities and differences between types of DSS.

The more DSS are used in an organization, the more important it is to draw distinctions between specific systems. Distinctions among systems can help ensure the correct decision support capability is provided to a specific need. Drawing meaningful distinctions can assist in understanding what specific type of DSS works and when.

In general, managers should continue to use the term *decision support system* when it facilitates understanding. DSS is not an archaic synonym for business intelligence (BI). Providing intelligence information to managers about the status, operations, and environment of a business is a worthwhile goal, and BI can be the purpose of a variety specific data-driven DSS. For some managers, it is probably tempting to change the terms used for information systems to stay current with vendor nomenclature. That strategy might work if all vendors agreed on terminology, but they do not, and it is important to resist the temptation. Maintaining an historical continuity in nomenclature and terminology helps make sense of what is observed and learned from research and experience.

Computing technologies used for building DSS are evolving and becoming more powerful and more sophisticated. Technologists are developing new systems to meet long-standing as well as newer needs derived from a more complex organizational environment. For those who build and try to understand computerized decision support, it is important to differentiate types of DSS in more elaborate and more meaningful ways. Adjectives such as Web-based, mobile, or data-driven should be used to enhance descriptions of systems.

In general, technologists should be more precise and more descriptive when discussing and describing a specific DSS. It is important to specify the purpose, targeted users, and technology. Are we investigating a data-driven, Web-based DSS for providing BI? Do we want a Web-based, document-driven DSS to assist in managing operational risk? Perhaps we want a spreadsheet-based, model-driven DSS for cost estimation.

What Is Analytics?

Analytics refers to quantitative analysis of data. Analytic capabilities are important in data-driven and model-driven DSS and analysis with quantitative and statistical tools is the focus of special studies such as knowledge discovery or data mining. There are three major types of analytics: (a) reporting analytics, (b) prescriptive analytics, and (c) predictive analytics.

Analytics is often described as the science of analysis and discovery. People who conduct analyses and develop analytic applications are decision or data scientists. Analytics refers to a broad set of information systems, tools, and capabilities that provide decision support.

Davenport and Harris[5] define analytics as "extensive use of data, statistical and quantitative analysis, exploratory and predictive models, and fact-based management to drive decisions and actions. The analytics may be input for human decisions or drive fully automated decisions" (p. 7).

Analytics relies on three main technologies: (a) data management and retrieval; (b) mathematical and statistical analysis and models; and (c) techniques for data visualization and display. Analytic applications are processing massive amounts of structured and unstructured data to find patterns and provide information.

Some sources consider analytics as a subset of BI, while others consider reporting analytics as another name for BI. In the remaining discussion, data-driven DSS and BI are considered reporting or data analytic applications. In general, BI is a product of business analytics. Data-driven systems provide BI and decision support. Prescriptive analytics manipulate large data sets to make recommendations. Predictive analytics are based on quantitative and statistical models and this category of analytics includes model-driven DSS. Analytics includes any type of computer supported analysis used to support fact-based decisions.

What Is Business Intelligence?

BI describes a set of concepts, methods, and technologies associated with fact-based support systems. The original purpose of BI systems was to increase access for managers and staff specialists to historical data for special studies and for periodic reporting.

Some managers view BI as a term similar to military or competitive intelligence. The presumed purpose of BI is to gather and provide information to help managers be more "intelligent" when making decisions. This interpretation of the term is appropriate for describing the activities of a staff group tasked with gathering and disseminating information, for example, a business intelligence unit, but it is confusing when explaining BI technologies and applications.

Information Systems vendors and analysts tend to use BI for a category of software tools that can be used to extract and analyze data from corporate databases. The most common BI software is query and reporting tools. This software extracts data from a database and creates formatted reports.

Business intelligence is a term used by some financial analysts and commentators to categorize a small group of software vendors and their products. Major BI tool vendors include: SAP/Business Objects, IBM/Cognos, Oracle-Hyperion, SAS, and MicroStrategy.

There are serious disagreements about the meaning of the term *Business Intelligence* and related terms such as *Business Intelligence Tools*. For example, Microsoft sells Excel and SQL Server with Pivot tables as BI products. IDC recognized Microsoft as one of the fastest-growing BI vendors.[6] Many would disagree with this categorization of Microsoft products.

SAP/Business Objects claims "business intelligence lets organizations access, analyze, and share information internally with employees and externally with customers, suppliers, and partners."

IBM-Cognos defines BI as "a category of applications and technologies for gathering, storing, analyzing, reporting on, and providing access to data to help enterprise users make better business decisions."

The IBM Developer Works glossary states, "Business Intelligence (BI) is the gathering, management and analysis of vast amounts of data in order to gain insights to drive strategic business decisions, and to support operational processes with new functions. BI is about the development of information that is conclusive, fact based, and actionable. It includes technology practices such as data warehouses, data marts, data mining, text mining, and on-line analytical processing (OLAP)."[7]

According to vendors, BI is some combination of their technologies and architectures producing timely information. Vendors are creating ambiguity and confusion with broad, catchall definitions and claims for BI. Consultants, IS/IT staff and managers often have differing and unrealistic views of BI. This confusion can be harmful. Managers need to know what they are buying when purchasing a BI product or system. In general, managers are buying a development platform for creating a data-driven DSS with a specific purpose of providing timely, company specific performance information.

What Is Operational Business Intelligence?

Managers want computerized information systems to provide facts to guide operational, day-to-day business decision making. Some vendors call such systems operational BI systems. Technology has improved and now it is much faster to capture, extract, load, and retrieve operational data to support real-time action taking and operational performance analysis and monitoring. Companies can build operational real-time DSS.

Many consultants and observers of BI applications such as Claudia Imhoff, Cindi Howson, and Ron Swift have identified operational BI as an important trend. Imhoff states that operational BI means "speeding up the analytics and embedding them in operational processes."[8]

Aberdeen Group,[9] a technology research and analysis firm, identifies six types of operational BI:

1. Transactional BI with analysis and reporting
2. Real-time analytics with business rules applied to data as it is captured
3. Near real-time analytics, automated analysis generated from business rules
4. Operational reporting, automatically generated and often distributed

5. Business activity monitoring (BAM) or business process monitoring of activity and performance

6. Decision management, rules-based engines, integrated reporting and analytic applications to automate actions.

Supporting operational decision making and monitoring operations are twin goals of systems lumped together as operational BI systems. In general, operational BI provides time-sensitive, relevant information to operations managers and front-line, customer-facing employees to support daily work processes. These data-driven DSS differ from other DSS and BI systems in terms of purpose, targeted users, data latency, data detail, and availability.

Imhoff[10] concluded in a recent column, "business intelligence has 'invaded' the operational space in a big way, offering in-line analytics, real-time or near real-time decision-making support for all employees in the enterprise. Today's BI environment includes three forms of BI—strategic, tactical, and operational." She defines operational BI as focusing on managing and supporting daily business operations; the primary users are business analysts, line of business managers, customer-facing staff, and those in operational processes. Imhoff identifies a shorter "intra-day" time span for operational BI than the monthly or quarterly time span of traditional BI.

What are common application areas for operational data-driven BI systems? (a) Customer relationship management applications, such as preparing revised passenger schedules for passengers on a delayed plane or supporting call center staff making decisions;[11] (b) Direct sales, such as supporting a salesperson using a PDA to access operational BI; (c) Monitoring operations, for example, Suzuki uses dashboards to highlight warranty claim and external customer satisfaction data; (d) Consolidating data and creating alerts, for example, integrating customer reservations data and TSA lists and generating security alert lists.

For many years, we have had a goal of helping decision makers monitor events and make choices as events occur. Today we are seeing the "dawn of the real-time enterprise."[12] Mobile phones deliver data in real-time to managers, sales staff, and emergency personnel, companies have active data warehouses, extensive event data is recorded in real-time, and business analytics are available in real-time or "near real-time." There are many possibilities for on-line, real-time decision support.

Are BAM and BPM Decision Support Systems?

Some people in the field of IS/IT really like acronyms. BAM is *business activity monitoring*. BPM may refer to three different concepts: business performance management, business performance monitoring, and business process management. Vendors adopt the same acronym for different types of software. All three can provide decision support. Managers reading about BPM, or talking to vendors at a trade show, should determine which BPM is the topic of discussion.

Some vendors advertise business performance management as the next generation of BI. This BPM software improves business processes such as planning and forecasting in order to help managers define, measure, and manage performance against strategic goals. Management translates goals into key performance indicators (KPIs) that are monitored using computerized systems. Often, business performance management is really business performance monitoring. A computer-based dashboard is a major BPM or corporate performance management (CPM) tool. Vendors are selling a specialized product that can be used to create a specific data-driven DSS.

Business activity monitoring (BAM), according to vendor Tibco (www.tibco.com), "refers to the aggregation, analysis, and presentation of relevant and timely information about business activities inside your organization and involving your customers and partners." BAM is a real-time version of business performance management. BAM uses performance dashboards for customizing metrics, setting alerts, and drilling down to detailed data to support decision making.

BAM systems usually use a computer dashboard display to present data, but a BAM dashboard differs from those used by BI systems. BAM processes events in real-time and pushes data to the dashboard. BI dashboards refresh at predetermined intervals by polling or querying databases. Depending on the refresh interval selected, BAM and BI dashboards can be similar or can vary widely.[13] BAM is a special case of business performance monitoring. BAM and performance monitoring systems are special purpose data-driven DSS.

Business process management (BPM) refers to supporting current or new activities in business processes with technology. Managers are using software to create agile business processes, ensure consistency, and improve quality. Document-driven DSS, document transaction management, or document tracking with online approval and authorization support are technologies associated with business process management.

New acronyms continue to challenge and confuse technologists and managers. For example, business process intelligence (BPI) is a new term for tools to monitor, control, and optimize processes. Event-driven business process management (EDBPM) supposedly focuses on real-time process management. Making distinctions is useful for explaining the purpose of a new software product, but vendors should stop promoting new acronyms.

BAM, BPM, and CPM describe a purpose for a computerized, management DSS. BAM, BPM, and CPM are examples of operational BI. We need to describe our decision support needs rather than create more acronyms. If managers want a real-time, data-driven system for monitoring KPIs, then specify that need and build or buy a system to meet the need. Operational business decision support is much more practical with modern technologies.

What Is Knowledge Management?

Knowledge management (KM) promotes activities and processes to acquire, create, document, and share formal explicit knowledge and informal, implicit knowledge. Researchers identify two focuses of KM: (a) *Management of Information,* where knowledge is content that can be identified and handled in an information system, and (b) *Management of People,* where knowledge consists of processes, a complex set of dynamic skills, training systems, and know-how that is constantly changing.[14] This section focuses on using technology for knowledge creation and sharing to support decision making. Some KM practitioners have a much broader focus on managing all of the knowledge in an organization.

Barclay and Murray define KM abstractly as:

a business activity with two primary aspects: (1) Treating the knowledge component of business activities as an explicit concern of business reflected in strategy, policy, and practice at all levels of the organization. (2) Making a direct connection between an organization's intellectual assets—both explicit [recorded] and tacit [personal know-how]—and positive business results.[15]

KM involves identifying a group of people who have a need to share knowledge, developing technological support that enables knowledge-sharing, and creating a process for transferring and disseminating knowledge.

In a review of KM research, Alavi and Leidner noted that "management reporting systems, decision support systems, and executive support systems have all focused on the collection and dissemination" of codified, explicit organizational knowledge. "Groupware enables organizations to create intraorganizational memory in the form of both structured and unstructured information and to share this memory across time and space."[16]

Knowledge management systems (KMS) store and manage information in a variety of digital formats. The software may assist in knowledge capture, categorization, deployment, inquiry, discovery, or communication. Some DSS are KMSs too.

By 2002, some of the excitement and hyperbole about KM had ended. T.D. Wilson, a retired Information Systems Professor, concluded KM was:

an umbrella term for a variety of organizational activities, none of which are concerned with the management of knowledge. Those activities that are not concerned with the management of information are concerned with the management of work practices, in the expectation that changes in such areas as communication practice will enable information sharing.[17]

Martin Dugage, a KM expert, stated a few years ago, "KM initiatives have shifted from developing and deploying large IT infrastructures and collaborative portals to management education, consulting and much simpler and focused collaborative IT systems."[18]

The term *knowledge management* is ambiguous and there is insufficient agreement on substance. Excitement about KM possibilities did encourage managers to experiment with groupware, company Intranets, expert systems, Web-based directories, and various DSS. For example, KM technologies are an important delivery component of document-driven and knowledge-driven DSS. Decision support is a more modest and much narrower concept than KM.

In general, KM activities, especially those supported by IT, have been successful in many companies. Some managers perceived and reported initial performance gains, but competitors rapidly imitated KM projects. Many KM technology-supported activities, such as Web-based directories and frequently asked questions forums, are now used in many companies.

Companies routinely use information technologies to manage and disseminate knowledge to support decision makers. We need to better understand when it is most appropriate and cost effective to use information technology for KM. Perhaps a manager wants a system to help identify people who have specific knowledge and make that information available on an Intranet. How much will the system be used and by whom? Perhaps we want to build a knowledge-driven DSS for customer support staff. How much will it cost? What is the benefit? Better support? Fewer staff? Decision support often involves managing and codifying explicit organizational knowledge.

Do Executives Need Specialized Decision Support?

At least 35 years ago, some chief executive officers (CEOs) began directly using computer workstations to find their own information.[19] Companies developed specialized Executive Information Systems to support their senior managers. By the mid-1990s, these specialized systems were losing favor in IT departments and in corporate boardrooms. Some IT staff perceived that a system used only by executives was elitist, while others saw EIS and briefing books as hard to maintain, underused, and redundant with other systems, and some managers felt their EIS had low-quality data. Vendors and IT managers saw Web-based, enterprise-wide BI systems as a replacement for EIS.

The emphasis of an EIS was graphical displays and an easy-to-use interface that presented information from the corporate and possibly external databases. EIS often provided canned reports or briefing books to top-level executives. An EIS had strong self-service reporting and drill-down capabilities. The goal was to have executives as "hands-on" users of the EIS for E-mail, calendar, reading reports, finding information, and monitoring KPIs.[20]

IS/IT analysts should monitor and work to understand executive decision support needs. Decision support should be targeted to many user groups and executives need an information system capability that helps them find problems, identify opportunities, and forecast trends.

Executive information needs continue to converge with BI and data warehousing technologies in the marketplace. Initially, EIS used proprietary databases that required many staff people to update, maintain, and create. This approach was very expensive and hard to justify. Today, executives need the structured and unstructured internal and external data that can be stored in an enterprise-wide data warehouse.

Modern executive decision support should report key results in dashboards and scorecards. In addition, performance measures must be easy to understand and monitor. Modern decision support should not add substantially to the workload of managers or staff, rather dedicated capabilities should add value in terms of improved decision making.

Specialized capabilities should be part of a Web-based, enterprise-wide, data-driven DSS that helps senior managers analyze, compare, and highlight trends in key variables. A proprietary, secure capability can store specialized reports, PowerPoint slides, and provide tools to monitor KPIs. Modern executive decision support should provide timely delivery of secure, sensitive, decision-relevant company information. Any system should provide filters and drill-down to reduce data overload. Modern decision support can increase the effectiveness of executive decision makers.

Executives and senior managers should be an important targeted user group for needed corporate information. Some executives would say they are the most important user group. So what decision support do executives need today? Modern EIS? Decision Intelligence Systems?[21] Portals? Or executive user views in an enterprise-wide data warehouse? Managers should explore needs and commit resources to build appropriate decision support capabilities.

Conclusions and Summary

In general, DSS is a class or category of computerized information system that supports decision-making activities. Figure 2.1 indicates the overlap and differences among decision support concepts. KM, decision support, DSS, analytics, and BI are broad, related general terms. Analytics and business analytics are terms that prescribe quantitative analysis of data. Reporting or data analytic applications include data-driven DSS and BI. Prescriptive analytics process large data sets to make recommendations. Predictive analytics use quantitative and statistical models for many tasks including targeting customers, estimating costs, and optimizing resource utilization. Predictive analytics are examples of model-driven decision support.

Specialized analytics, BI, and DSS provide decision support; we also can use computers and analytic software in special studies and we can use software to automate decisions. Reporting analytics and BI refers to systems that use historical or real-time data and are classified as data-driven DSS. Operational BI systems are intended for use by operations decision

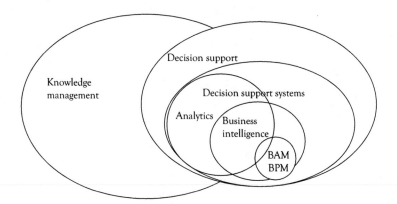

Figure 2.1. Decision support concept map.

makers. BAM and various types of BPM are special purpose types of operational BI. Executives still need specialized information and decision support. Managers should expect that vendors will continue to invent new terms and acronyms. Perhaps the expanded framework discussed in the next chapter will provide an ongoing, systematic means to describe decision support capabilities.

CHAPTER 3

Recognizing Types of Decision Support

For thousands of years, people have used decision aids, such as checklists, to help in decision making. Record keeping is a way to have historical data for decision making. Building scale models was and is a tool to help in planning. Using signal fires for warning in times of war was a tool for communications and decision support. In many ways, we write technical books to codify knowledge for the next generation of decision makers. The world has changed, and now, more than ever before, managers need more sophisticated computerized tools for decision support.

In the last 30 years, researchers have created frameworks for classifying decision support systems (DSS). In 1980, Alter categorized DSS in terms of generic operations ranging from extremely data-oriented to extremely model-oriented systems. In 1996, Holsapple and Whinston identified five specialized types of DSS, including text-oriented, database-oriented, spreadsheet-oriented, solver-oriented, and rule-oriented. In 2005, Arnott and Pervan traced the evolution of DSS using seven categories: personal DSS, group support systems, negotiation support systems, intelligent DSS, knowledge management-based DSS, executive information systems/business intelligence, and data warehousing.[1]

This chapter provides an overview of the types of decision support and summarizes a modern, systematic decision support framework that can help you better describe decision support needs. An organizing framework can help identify similarities and differences in solutions to decision support needs.

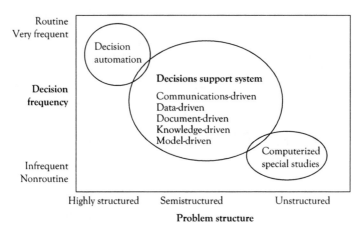

Figure 3.1. Decision support spectrum: Matching decision support to the situation.

What Are Current Decision Support Possibilities?

Decision support is a broad concept that prescribes using computerized systems and other tools to assist in individual, group, and organization decision making. We use decision support tools routinely in a specific decision process. We use tools such as Microsoft Excel to help make an especially difficult decision. In addition, we write programs to implement business rules to automate decisions. We use many different decision support systems.

At one end of the decision support spectrum are tools for making or automating decisions—this is the realm of decision automation. At the unstructured, nonroutine end of the decision support spectrum, we create tools for one-time special studies. In the decision support spectrum, if a human decision maker is in the decision-making process as the "decider," then either we are using a DSS or we are conducting a computer-supported special study (see Figure 3.1).

What Is Decision Automation?

The concept of decision automation is deceptively simple and intriguingly complex. We are using information technologies to make decisions and implement programmed decision processes. Decision automation is most appropriate for well-structured, clearly defined, routine, or programmed decision situations.[2]

An automated decision process occurs without any human intervention. We program decision-making procedures using algorithms based on quantitative models, logical or quantitative heuristics, statistical methods, or artificial intelligence technologies. Once in operation, the programs evaluate stored or real-time data from sensors. On the basis of data inputs and program analytics, one or more actions result. For example, a rule may change the value in a database, send a message or an alert, move an object, or play a message.

Human decision makers determine the rules, models, and methods used for making choices and completing decision tasks in programmed decision situations. Decision automation is a set of concepts, a related set of technologies, a set of methods and design tools, and an ambitious, general goal. The range of decision tasks we can automate has increased because of improved technologies and design tools. This technology evolution has also raised aspiration levels and created more challenging development goals. The overriding goal is to replace human decision makers in programmable decision situations where a computer decision is at least as good as that of most human decision makers. The working assumption is that decision automation will be cost effective when compared to an equally skilled human decision maker in a programmed decision situation. The popularized term *enterprise decision management* (EDM) refers to automating operational decisions using business rules software with predictive analytics. The goal of EDM is to automate and improve high-volume operational decisions.[3]

The greatly expanded and evolving computing infrastructure makes it increasingly cost effective to apply decision automation in situations where it had been prohibitively costly. The role of a human decision maker is usually limited to handling exceptions and periodically revising business rules.

What Is a Computer-Supported Special Study?

In unstructured, nonroutine decision situations, we often use computer applications for one-time special studies—this is the realm of management scientists, financial analysts, and marketing researchers. We can support these unstructured, nonroutine situations with computerized systems, but the support focuses on information retrieval, presentation, summarization, and quantitative analyses. Managers may define information needs, but specialists often develop a computerized analysis to provide the needed information. For example, a manager may be concerned about customer turnover and request a special study to identify characteristics of customers who are loyal and frequent buyers and those who are not. The study may involve data mining, statistical analysis, and possibly additional data collection.

We often develop computerized quantitative models as part of a decision support special study. We sometimes incorrectly identify these applications as DSS. In most cases in a special study, the application user interface in not as sophisticated and feature laden as is one found in a DSS. Examples of one-time special studies that use models include merger and acquisition analyses, lease versus purchase decisions, new venture analyses, capital budgeting, and equipment replacement decisions. When classifying computer applications, applying the seven characteristics of a DSS discussed in this chapter can help avoid classifying model-based special studies as model-driven DSS.

Special studies use a broad range of computerized decision support. A manager may conduct a one-time analysis using Excel, a marketing researcher may use a data-mining tool for a market basket analysis, or a financial analyst may conduct a cost–benefit analysis for a new product.

What Are the Different Types of DSS?

In the middle of the decision support spectrum is the broad realm of computerized DSS. These systems support recurring, semistructured decision processes. This section explains a DSS framework or typology with one major dimension and three secondary dimensions (i.e., purpose, targeted users, and enabling technology). The major dimension is the dominant architecture component that defines five types of DSS. The types of DSS include (a) communications-driven; (b) data-driven; (c) document-driven; (d) knowledge-driven; and (e) model-driven DSS.[4]

Communications-driven DSS emphasize communicating, collaborating, and shared decision-making support using technology. A simple bulletin board or threaded E-mail is the most elementary level of functionality. Groupware is a subset of a broader concept called collaborative computing. Communications-driven DSS enable two or more people to communicate with each other, share information, and coordinate their activities. Group decision support systems (GDSS) may be either primarily communications-driven or primarily model-driven DSS. Some GDSS allow multiple users to work collaboratively using various software tools. Examples of group support tools used in communications-driven DSS include audio conferencing, bulletin boards, Web conferencing, virtual worlds, computer-supported face-to-face meeting software, and interactive video. The dominant architecture component is communications capabilities.

Data-driven DSS emphasize access to and manipulation of a time-series of internal company data and in some systems real-time and external data. Simple file systems accessed by query and retrieval tools provide reporting functionality. Data warehouse systems provide access to larger amounts of data and additional functionality. A system with analytical processing provides the highest level of functionality. Business intelligence systems for operational or strategic use are most often data driven. BAM and BPM data-driven DSS use real-time data to assist in operational performance monitoring. The dominant component in these systems is the capture, storage, and retrieval of structured data.

Document-driven DSS integrate a variety of storage and processing technologies to provide complete document retrieval and analysis. Examples of documents include policies and procedures, product specifications, catalog content, minutes of meetings, corporate records, and important correspondence. A search engine is a powerful decision-aiding tool associated with a document-driven DSS. A document-driven DSS is one type of knowledge management system. Documents and document management provide the functionality for this type of DSS.

Knowledge-driven DSS suggest or recommend actions to managers. These DSS are person–computer systems with specialized problem-solving expertise. These systems store and apply knowledge for a variety of specific business problems. These problems include classification and configuration tasks such as loan approval, help desk support, risk management, and application of company policies. A knowledge-driven DSS uses artificial intelligence and statistical technologies. Knowledge storage and processing technologies are the dominant component in the architecture for these systems.

Model-driven DSS emphasize access to and manipulation of a quantitative model (e.g., an algebraic, financial, optimization, or simulation model). Simple analytical tools based on an algebraic model provide the most elementary level of functionality. Model-driven DSS use data and parameters provided by decision makers to aid them in analyzing a situation, but they are not usually data intensive. Quantitative models provide the functionality for this type of system. Users may input the data or retrieve data from a specialized database.

Not all decision situations require, nor would managers and groups benefit from, computerized decision support. The key for managers and developers is to have a shared framework for discussing wants and needs. The realm of computerized decision support continues to expand to more and more decision situations. In general, computerized decision support promotes rational decision behavior that uses analytical decision processes. Where the situation does not require, expect, encourage, or need analysis, then computerized decision support is unnecessary.

Computerized decision support should be considered when managers are in decision situations characterized by one or more of the following factors: complexity, relevant knowledge, uncertainty, specific goals, multiple groups with a stake in the decision outcome (multiple stakeholders), a large amount of information (especially company data or documents), or rapid change in information, or any combination of these factors.

Table 3.1 summarizes the expanded framework for specifying and classifying DSS. In addition to identifying the dominant component in the DSS architecture and type of DSS, it is important to specify the purpose of the proposed system, the targeted users, and proposed technology for deploying the DSS. For example, do you want a communications-driven DSS that supports globally distributed project teams using Web 2.0 technologies? Perhaps the need is for data-driven DSS with real-time data that tracks performance from a company's stores for a traveling district manager using a smartphone.

Table 3.1. An Expanded DSS Framework

DSS type	Dominant DSS component	Targeted user (examples)	Purpose (examples)	Enabling technology (examples)
Communications-driven DSS	Communications	Internal teams	Conduct a meeting	Bulletin board
		Supply chain partners	Help user collaborate	Videoconferencing
				Virtual worlds
Data-driven DSS	Database	Managers and staff, now suppliers	Query a data warehouse	Relational databases
				Multidimensional databases
Document-driven DSS	Document storage and management	Specialists and user group are expanding	Search web pages	Search engines, HTML
Knowledge-driven DSS	Knowledge base, AI	Internal users, now customers	Management advice	Expert system
Model-driven DSS	Quantitative models	Managers and staff, now customers	Scheduling	Linear programming, Excel
			Forecasting	

What Are the Basic Characteristics of a DSS?

Alter identified three major characteristics of DSS that remain current and relevant:

1. DSS are designed specifically to facilitate decision processes.
2. DSS should support rather than automate decision making.
3. DSS should be able to respond quickly to the changing needs of decision makers.[5]

Holsapple and Whinston identified characteristics one should expect to observe in a DSS. Their list is very general and provides an even broader perspective of the DSS concept. They specify that a DSS must have four characteristics: (a) DSS must have a body of knowledge; (b) DSS need a record-keeping capability that can present knowledge on an ad hoc basis in various customized ways as well as in standardized reports; (c) DSS should have capabilities for selecting a desired subset of stored knowledge for either presentation or for deriving new knowledge; (d) DSS must be designed to interact directly with a decision maker in such a way that the user has a flexible choice and sequence of knowledge-management activities.[6]

Many have tried to narrow the "population of systems" called DSS. For example, Turban and Aronson define 13 characteristics and capabilities of DSS. Their first characteristic is:

DSS provide support for decision makers mainly in semi-structured and unstructured situations by bringing together human judgment and computerized information. Such problems cannot be solved (or cannot be solved conveniently) by other computerized systems or by standard quantitative methods or tools.[7]

Their list is a useful starting point for defining characteristics of the class of information systems called DSS.

A consistent definition of DSS and a set of characteristics should improve communications about decision support. A characteristic of a DSS is an observable feature, property, or attribute of any type of DSS that differentiates a DSS from any other type of computer-based information system. Defining characteristics should help people recognize and identify a DSS.

The following are the primary or basic characteristics of a computerized DSS:

1. *Facilitation.* DSS facilitate and support specific decision-making activities or decision processes, or both.
2. *Interaction.* DSS are computer-based systems designed for interactive use by decision makers or staff users who control the sequence of interaction and the operations performed.
3. *Ancillary.* DSS can support decision makers at any level in an organization. They are not intended to replace decision makers.
4. *Repeated Use.* DSS are intended for repeated use. A specific DSS may be used routinely or used as needed for ad hoc decision support tasks.
5. *Task Oriented.* DSS provide specific capabilities that support one or more tasks related to decision making, including intelligence and data analysis, identification and design of alternatives, choice among alternatives, and decision implementation.
6. *Identifiable.* DSS may be independent systems that collect or replicate data from other information systems or subsystems of a larger, more integrated information system.
7. *Decision Impact.* DSS are intended to improve the accuracy, timeliness, quality, and overall effectiveness of a specific decision or a set of related decisions.

In addition to knowing we want a DSS, we must ask, "What features do we want in the proposed DSS?" Often, DSS design is similar to purchasing a new car with many customizable features. First, get the intended users to decide on their needs, then find a basic type or model that is a good fit, and finally get the users to identify and evaluate "must have" and "desirable" features so that a cost trade-off can occur. Finally, we build and customize the specific system. To assist in this process, let us now examine features of the five types of DSS.

What Are the Features of a
Communications-Driven DSS?

Features are an attribute of a DSS that may or may not confer a user benefit. A specific communications-driven DSS will not necessarily have all of the features associated with this general category of DSS, but a list of features helps specify computerized decision support needs and wants.

Many identifiable features are found in products variously known as *electronic meeting software, groupware, GDSS, conferencing software,* and *collaborative software* that can be used to create powerful communications-driven DSS. Over the years, the technical possibilities have expanded with the development of video and voice over the Internet protocol. Web-based chat and instant messaging software appeared in the mid-1990s. In the late 1990s, the company PlaceWare created the first Web conferencing capability and Microsoft introduced NetMeeting. Communications-driven DSS use communications technologies to facilitate collaboration, communication, and decision making. Communications technologies are central to supporting decision making in these systems.

A communications-driven DSS may support synchronous (same time) or asynchronous (different time) communications and meetings or both types. A specific system may support two-party or multiparty communications and decision making. Usually, communications-driven DSS are purchased applications. The lowest level of asynchronous, communications-driven decision support comes from E-mail. Threaded bulletin boards with polling provide more functionality. The lowest level of synchronous, communications-driven decision support comes from voice telephony. Dedicated video conferencing provides more functionality.

The architecture for communications-driven DSS may involve a distributed deployment model or a centralized deployment. The focus may be on desktop, team-oriented systems, distributed "boardrooms," or Web-based deployments. The major constraint when video conferencing or a virtual world is included in the architecture is the bandwidth and capacity of the system.

Based on research and experience, the following is an alphabetical list of five major features:

1. *Agenda Creation.* Virtual decision-making meetings are more productive with an agenda of issues and tasks. Ideally, a communications-driven DSS will facilitate creating and following an agenda.
2. *Application and Document Sharing.* During a meeting, participants should be able to easily share analyses, documents, PowerPoint slides, and so forth. Exchanging ideas by posting messages to a Web-based bulletin board can be a useful asynchronous decision support tool.
3. *Interaction.* Using chat, voice or video interaction in real-time conversation between people online is a key feature. Seeing and hearing participants during a virtual meeting expands the social interaction and can facilitate team building and acceptance of a shared decision. The type of interaction should depend on technology and situational factors.
4. *Polls.* During a meeting, it can be useful for the team leader to conduct a vote on a topic or gather opinions.
5. *Record Meetings.* Communications-driven DSS should have some capability to record inputs and ideally a team leader should be able to record the entire meeting for replay and review.

Vendors claim video conferencing software can raise productivity, reduce travel expenses, build stronger relationships with remote staff, and use limited resources more effectively. A communications-driven DSS should have these benefits and should reduce the cycle time for shared decision making, increase accountability, improve acceptance of shared decisions, and facilitate implementation of decisions in a distributed organization.

The cost of deploying a low-end, synchronous, communications-driven DSS can be as little as the cost of a Webcam for each participant to many thousands of dollars for more sophisticated deployments. We can deploy bulletin boards inexpensively for asynchronous decision support and knowledge management.

What Are the Features of a Data-Driven DSS?

Early data-oriented DSS displayed data based on criteria, made simple calculations, displayed reports and tables, and plotted scatter diagrams. The primary use of the systems was ad hoc reporting, budget consolidation, corporate performance monitoring, and revenue yield analysis. Research on Executive Information Systems expanded the features managers expect from data-driven DSS.[8] A major advance in technical capabilities of data-driven DSS occurred in the early 1990s with the introduction of data warehouses and Online Analytical Processing (OLAP) software.

The key to a successful data-driven DSS is having easy and rapid access to a large amount of accurate, well-organized multidimensional data. Codd and colleagues argued that OLAP systems were characterized by multidimensional conceptual view, links to a variety of data sources, ease for users to access and understand, and provide multiuser support, intuitive data manipulation, flexible reporting, and analytical capabilities.[9]

The following is an alphabetical list of five major features of data-driven DSS from a user's perspective:

1. *Ad hoc Data Filtering and Retrieval.* The system helps users search for and retrieve structured data; filtering often uses drop down menus, queries are often predefined, and users have drill-down capabilities. Drill down means looking at highly summarized data initially and optionally examining the most detailed data.
2. *Alerts and Triggers.* Systems may help users establish rules for E-mail notification and for other predefined actions when data change.
3. *Create Data Displays.* Users can usually choose among displays like scatter diagrams, bar and pie charts, and can often interactively change the displays.
4. *Data Management and Summarization.* Users can view or create pivot tables and cross tabulations. Users can create custom aggregations and calculate computed fields, totals, and subtotals. A pivot table summarizes selected fields and rows of data in a table format. Many data-driven DSS let users extract and download data for further analysis in a tool like Microsoft Excel, while some systems allow users to upload data for analysis in a user's working storage.

5. *View Predefined Data Displays and Production Reports.* DSS design-ers may create and store predefined, periodic reports as part of a data-driven DSS for users to access. For example, a system for opera-tional performance monitoring often includes a dashboard display. A system for more long-term strategic performance monitoring often includes a scorecard display.

Overall, with a well-designed data-driven DSS, managers can access a single version of the truth about company activities, perform their own analyses, have access to reliable, consistent, and high-quality information, make better-informed decisions, and have more timely information. To achieve good results, we need to build an appropriate DSS data store, cre-ate a user interface with desired features, institute effective data govern-ance, and ensure consistent data gathering. In addition, managers need to be willing to share and integrate data across the enterprise.

What Are the Features of a Document-Driven DSS?

Document-driven DSS often use the same document storage system as the document creator used in his or her workflow. This means the DSS designer is building a subsystem and must work with all of the constraints associated with the broader document management or content manage-ment system (CMS) environment.

Vannevar Bush's 1945 article in the *Atlantic Monthly* created a chal-lenging vision for managing documents and augmenting people's mem-ory. Bush wrote:

> Consider a future device for individual use, which is a sort of mech-anized private file and library. It needs a name, and, to coin one at random, "memex" will do. A memex is a device in which an indi-vidual stores all his books, records, and communications, and which is mechanized so that it may be consulted with exceeding speed and flexibility. It is an enlarged intimate supplement to his memory.[10]

Bush's memex is a much broader vision than is possible with current document-driven DSS.

Document-driven DSS help people use digitized, unstructured content in decision making. The features and technologies available for designing a document-driven DSS are becoming more common in products and more sophisticated.

A *content management system* is a computer software system used to assist users in the process of managing content. CMS facilitates the organization, control, and publication of a large set of documents and other content, such as images and multimedia resources. A CMS often facilitates the collaborative creation of documents. Some CMS also include workflow software support. Many CMS-supported tasks are transaction processing rather than decision support, but the software often includes capabilities and features that are useful for building a document-driven decision support subsystem. Part of the design of a document-driven DSS is indexing and organization of documents. A document-driven DSS can assist in monitoring decision process status, routing of decision-relevant information, and recording of decisions.

Bush's vision of a "memex" identified some key features and capabilities that the system would provide users. His list served as a starting point for developing a list of features for document-driven DSS. The following are five major features from a user's perspective:

1. *Ad hoc Search and Retrieval.* Users can enter their own search terms, use stored queries, and the system often has a search interface that is easy for a user to apply logical operators. The results are often ranked for relevance.

2. *Browsing and Document Navigation.* Browsing is an interactive capability that lets a user explore the document collection. The system may provide for rapid scanning of a document. An index may include an alphabetical listing of key words, names, or topics, or all.

3. *Document Management.* Users have limited "working storage" for comments, links, and ratings. Some systems have document check-in and check-out.

4. *Summarization.* The system provides extracts of a document using statistical cues like word frequency to form summaries.

5. *Text Mining and Text Analysis.* Some software attempts to extract patterns from natural language text. Also, a system may have a capability for comparing multiple versions of a document for differences.

Document retrieval is a key capability that focuses on how people can find needed documents and how much time they spend looking for them. In many situations, we can reduce the cost of retrieval for decision-relevant documents with a well-designed document-driven DSS.

The prospects and benefits for managing knowledge and supporting decision making using document-driven DSS is evolving and expanding. The Web has made document databases easier to access. Managers can perform their own searches and have more timely unstructured information. Managers need to carefully read and interpret the documents retrieved from the system, but new tools help in text mining and analysis. To build sophisticated document-driven DSS, designers need to organize documents and preplan indexes, create a user interface with desired features, and institute effective document governance and management.

What Are the Features of a Knowledge-Driven DSS?

In general, a knowledge-driven DSS suggests or recommends actions to targeted users. Other terms used for this purpose include *advisory systems, consultation systems, suggestion systems, knowledge-based systems, recommender systems, rule-based DSS,* and *management expert systems.*[11]

Knowledge-driven DSS can store and apply knowledge for a variety of specific problems and tasks. The generic tasks include classification, configuration, diagnosis, interpretation, planning, and prediction. Historically, diagnosis has been the most popular DSS application area. Building a specific knowledge-driven DSS depends on the demand for the system and the anticipated benefits. As with all DSS, the goal is to support a human decision maker in completing a task requiring domain-specific knowledge, rather than replacing the decision maker. The programming and development tools used to build these systems are based on Artificial Intelligence and Statistics. The systems may be rule-based, statistics-based, heuristic, object-based, logic-based, or induction-based. Some systems use more than one technology.

Classification involves separating a specific instance into a broader class based on characteristics. Configuration involves creating an arrangement of objects given performance criteria or constraints. Diagnosis involves hypothesizing a cause given symptom and situational information. Interpretation refers to adding meaning, explanation, and possibly understanding in a specific situation or context. Planning usually involves sequencing an assortment of actions or means to achieve desired ends in a constrained situation. Finally, prediction refers to identifying and forecasting a future state of a system.

A major barrier to progress with building these systems is the ability to make the knowledge readily available. In recent years, Web technologies as well as handheld and tablet PCs have made deployment of knowledge-driven DSS much easier and much less expensive.

The following are six major features of knowledge-driven DSS from a user's perspective:

1. *Asks Questions.* Historically, knowledge-driven DSS attempt to create an interactive dialogue with users to simulate an interrogation by a "real" expert. A key feature is interactivity with the user and contingent branching based on responses. This capability is often in the form of a Yes/No or multiple-choice question.

2. *Backtrack Capability.* Users can often move backward through the questions and alter responses. This feature makes it possible to change a subjective judgment and hence change a recommendation or result.

3. *Display Confidence or Certainty Information.* Some systems calculate numeric values called confidences, likelihoods, or ranks. A confidence interval is a statistical range with a specified probability that a given result lies within the range. The DSS may be able to create a confidence interval for a recommendation or diagnosis.

4. *Explain How and Why.* After a knowledge-driven DSS has reached a solution or conclusion for a problem, a user can often request an explanation. This is one of the most powerful features and is common in a knowledge-driven DSS. Also, users should be able to ask why the system is asking a specific question. These features can enhance user confidence in the recommendation and hence acceptance of the system.

5. *Initiate Actions.* In some knowledge-driven DSS, users can send an E-mail or otherwise implement a recommendation.

6. *Retrieve Data About a Specific Case or Instance.* Data used in some knowledge-driven DSS may come from other computerized sources and users must be able to retrieve data from external sources. For example, a diagnostic system may retrieve information about a patient from laboratory tests or a configuration system may need data from an inventory system.

The prospects and benefits for managing knowledge and supporting decision making using knowledge-driven DSS are evolving. These DSS can increase the distribution of expertise, broaden job descriptions for individual workers, and create a new communication channel for knowledge. Using a knowledge-driven DSS can result in more consistent decisions and can create efficiencies and reduce the time needed to solve problems. These DSS can also reduce training costs and rapidly update knowledge. Finally, an enterprise-wide knowledge-driven DSS can help centralize control of repetitive, semi-structured decision-making processes.

What Are the Features of a Model-Driven DSS?

In general, a model-driven DSS provides access to and manipulation of a quantitative model. Model-driven DSS may have multiple subsystems that use various models.

A DSS that helps prepare monthly or quarterly budget forecasts probably uses an accounting model. Simulation is the most commonly used tool for studying dynamic systems. For example, a store manager may use simulation in a DSS with an inventory model to determine order quantities. Optimization systems help estimate the results for various decision alternatives given a set of constraints. Linear programming is the most widely used optimization technique. A typical DSS application of linear programming involves resource allocation. We often use simulation methods and optimization models in special decision support studies.

We use model-driven DSS to assist in formulating alternatives, analyzing impacts of alternatives, and interpreting and selecting appropriate options. Examples of tasks supported with model-driven DSS include crew deployment, job scheduling, advertising allocation, forecasting product usage, cost estimation and pricing, tax planning, and investment analysis.

The following are the major features of a model-driven DSS:

1. *Change a Model Parameter or "What If" Analysis.* Performing a "what if" analysis involves varying a single model input parameter over a reasonable range. This is a major feature of model-driven DSS. For example, we use a slider to adjust values in a range. Also, users often want to determine the impact of systematic changes in the values of one or two variables over a reasonable range on the results of a model. In Excel, one and two variable data tables provide sensitivity analysis.

2. *Create and Manage Scenarios.* A scenario is a specified combination of values assigned to one or more variable cells in a model. Scenarios can involve many decision variables. Some model-driven DSS have predefined scenarios while other systems make it easy for users to add and modify scenarios.

3. *Extract Specific Historical Data Values from an External Database.* For example, a model-driven DSS for investment analysis may provide a capability to extract historical stock information from a database.

4. *Output Selection.* Model-driven DSS usually have multiple formats for displaying outputs. For example, it may be possible to select a pie or a bar chart. Some DSS based on simulation provide a visual animation.

5. *Specify and Seek Goals.* Goal seek is a capability for specifying the desired result of a model and working backward to identify decisions to reach the goal. When using goal seek in Excel, the value in a specific cell is varied until the formula that is dependent on that cell returns the desired result.

6. *Value Elicitation and Data Input.* There are three primary approaches for collecting user input and eliciting values: (a) asking for a number;

(b) using a graphical device like a slider; and (c) asking for a word or verbal input like high or low. Model-driven DSS use all of these approaches.

A quantitative model is an abstraction of relationships in a complex situation. We need to monitor the results of using a specific model-driven DSS carefully for ongoing validity and usefulness. If the model is incomplete, inaccurate, or misspecified, the results from it can adversely influence a decision maker's judgment.

What Type of DSS Is the System or Subsystem?

Managers and developers now recognize that products and systems advertized as business intelligence, decision support systems, or knowledge management systems do not solve the same problem. The message is getting out that DSS are not identical in features and capabilities. DSS researchers have observed and recognized the differences for many years, but now managers, developers, and vendors realize that differentiation or categorization of DSS is important.

Classification of objects, things, and artifacts is partly a systematic analysis and partly the application of specific criteria from a rubric linked to a classification scheme. Many of us have played the game "20 Questions" during our youth, or as parents with our children. The game is fun, low cost, and educational and it teaches classification skills. Often times the player begins with a question like "Is it a plant, animal, or mineral?" The 20 questions elicit information about the object and help determine what it is. When classifying specific DSS or DSS generators, we can use a 20-questions approach.

After you have gathered as much information as possible on a vendor's product or a system used in a company that someone calls a DSS, then ask the questions in Table 3.2 to categorize the DSS.

When in doubt about which type of DSS you have or want, collect more information and ask more questions. You may actually want a DSS with multiple, integrated subsystems. For strategic issues like improving computerized decision support, an organization benefits when a shared vocabulary is used.

Table 3.2. **Categorizing DSS**

Question	Conclusion
1. Does the system support decision making?	*If NO, stop.*
2. Does the system have multiple identifiable subsystems?	*If YES, focus on one subsystem.*
3. Does the system have the characteristics of a DSS?	*If YES, then a DSS.*

4. Does electronic communication provide decision support functionality?
  a. Does use of the DSS involve either synchronous or asynchronous collaboration?
  b. Do tools facilitate communications about a decision situation?
	If all answers to question 4 and its subpoints are YES, conclude communications-driven DSS.

5. Does the DSS include a large, structured database of historical data?
  a. Can users query and interact with the data?
  b. Are real-time data updates a component of the application?
  c. Are predefined reports available to users?
  d. Is data displayed on a map or geographic representation?
  e. Does functionality come from rapid access and analysis of data?
	If answers to questions 5 and 5.e. are YES, and YES to some of 5. a. through 5.d., conclude data-driven DSS.

6. Does the DSS include a large database of unstructured documents?
  a. Can users search, retrieve, summarize, and sort documents?
  b. Are documents used in a decision?
  c. Does document retrieval and analysis provide functionality?
	If all answers to question 6 and its subpoints are YES, conclude document-driven DSS.

7. Does the DSS score and codify knowledge or expertise?
  a. Is human expertise stored using AI technologies?
  b. Does the DSS provide recommendations or advice?
  c. Does expert support provide functionality?
	If all answers to question 7 and its subpoints are YES, conclude knowledge-driven DSS.

8. Does the DSS include one or more quantitative models?
  a. Can users manipulate the model with "what if" analysis?
  b. Does the interactive model analysis provide functionality?
	If all answers to question 8 and its subpoints are YES, conclude mode-driven DSS.

Summary

This chapter examined the decision support spectrum, including decision automation, types of decision support systems, and computer-supported special studies. The five more specific DSS types are communications-driven, data-driven, document-driven, knowledge-driven, and model-driven DSS. DSS facilitate and support specific decision-making activities and decision processes.

The first three chapters have focused on basic concepts and on creating a shared vocabulary and framework for categorizing DSS. The next chapter examines a specific category of DSS—business intelligence and data-driven DSS.

CHAPTER 4

Business Intelligence and Data-Driven DSS

Most managers want to make fact-based decisions. Many large organizations have implemented database systems called data warehouses (DW) to organize facts for timely retrieval. Some organizations have implemented business intelligence (BI) systems based on earlier management and executive information systems (EIS). BI refers to extracting, analyzing, and distributing data from corporate databases to support decision making. For many years, the prospects and problems of providing managers with timely management information have been discussed and debated. Overall, managers and information systems specialists seem interested in learning more about new types of data-driven decision support systems (DSS). So the debate about costs, advantages, problems, and possibilities for data-driven decision support must continue.

As noted in Chapter 2, the expanded DSS framework categorizes DW, EIS, Spatial DSS, and BI systems as data-driven DSS. Some authors include data mining as data-driven decision support. Analytics is used as an umbrella term for data- and model-driven DSS and various BI capabilities.

Data-driven DSS and BI systems are often very expensive to develop and implement in organizations. Despite the large resource commitments that are required, many companies have implemented data-driven DSS. Technologies are changing and managers and MIS staff will need to make continuing investments in this category of DSS software. Hence it is important that managers understand the various terms and systems that use large databases to support management decision making.

Gartner and Forester analysts[1] forecast positive developments for BI by 2015, including (a) 15% of BI deployments will combine BI, collaboration, and social software into decision-making environments and (b) 33% of BI functionality will be delivered to handheld devices.

This chapter discusses 11 important questions related to BI and data-driven decision support.

What Is Data Warehousing?

Managers need to be familiar with some data warehousing and BI terminology (the basic "what is" questions) and they need to have an idea of the benefits and limitations of these decision support components (the "why" questions). More technical people in Information Systems need to know how and when to develop systems using these components.

A data warehouse (DW) is a database designed to support a broad range of decision tasks in a specific organization. It is usually batch updated and structured for rapid online queries and managerial summaries. DW contain large amounts of historical data. The term *data warehousing* is often used to describe the process of creating, managing, and using a DW.

The terms *data warehousing* and *OLAP* are often used interchangeably. As the definitions suggest, warehousing refers to the organization and storage of data from a variety of sources so that it can be analyzed and retrieved easily. OLAP deals with the software and the process of analyzing data, managing aggregations, and partitioning information into cubes for in-depth analysis, retrieval, and visualization. Some vendors are replacing the term *OLAP* with the terms *analytical software* and *business intelligence.*

DW or a more focused database called a *data mart* should be considered when a significant number of potential users are requesting access to a large amount of related historical information for analysis and reporting purposes. So-called active or real-time DW can provide advanced decision support capabilities.

In general, organized data about business transactions and business operations is stored in a DW. But, any data used to manage a business or any type of data that has value to a business should be evaluated for storage in the warehouse. Some static data may be compiled for initial loading into the warehouse. Any data that comes from mainframe, client/server, or Web-based systems can then be periodically loaded into the warehouse. The idea behind a DW is to capture and maintain useful data in a central location. Once data is organized, managers and analysts can use software tools such as OLAP to link different types of data together and potentially turn that data into valuable information that can be used for a variety of business decision support needs, including analysis, discovery, reporting, and planning.

Normalization of a relational database for transaction processing avoids processing anomalies and results in the most efficient use of database storage. A DW for decision support is not intended to achieve these same goals. For data-driven decision support, the main concern is to provide information to the user as fast as possible. Because of this, storing data in a denormalized manner, including storing redundant data and presummarizing data, provides the best retrieval results. In addition, DW data is usually static so anomalies will not occur from operations such as add, delete, and update of a record or field.

The best way to get started with data warehousing is to analyze some existing transaction processing systems and see what type of historical trends and comparisons might be interesting to examine to support decision making. See if there is a "real" user need for integrating that data. If there is, then IS/IT staff can develop a data model for a new schema and load it with some current data and start creating a decision support data store using a database management system (DBMS). Then they can use software for query and reporting and build a decision support interface that is easy to use. Although the initial DW/data-driven DSS may seem to meet only limited needs, it is a "first step." Start small and build more sophisticated systems based on experience and success rates.

What Questions Are Important for Evaluating a BI Data-Driven Decision Support Proposal?

Introducing a major project to provide enterprise-wide BI is much more than just another technology project. Often, the culture and decision-making processes must change to reward and reinforce fact-based decision making. Gartner, IBM Cognos, and many others have discussed questions to ask to help ensure "flawless business intelligence" or "avoid fatal flaws." Asking the right questions is important and a checklist helps improve system implementation and aids in discussions with vendors.

Prepare your questions in advance and consider asking the following seven key questions:

Question #1: What is the purpose of the proposed system? Reporting, ad hoc query and analysis, performance monitoring?

Question #2: Who wants the system? Will they really use it? Knowing who is promoting the project helps assess motivations and the possible acceptance of the system.

Question #3: Is there a data quality problem? How serious is the problem? A data-driven DSS cannot provide useful BI if there is a serious, significant, major data quality problem. Assessing what data is available and its quality early on avoids serious problems during development.

Question #4: What vendors are "best in class"? Are you wedded to your current vendor of a database for transaction systems? It is important to determine if there is a bias toward a specific vendor or development approach.

Question #5: Do you have a realistic schedule for the implementation process? Schedule feasibility is important to consider before committing to the project. An unrealistic implementation schedule is a major source of cost overruns and frustrations.

Question #6: Do you have inhouse staff to work on the project? If not, are you comfortable outsourcing to contractors or vendor staff a key decision support capability?

Question #7: Did the person suggesting the project just meet with a vendor or attend a tradeshow? Are they excited about dashboards? Or analytics?

Please ask these questions and review the answers carefully as part of a feasibility study. If the resulting decision is to proceed with a project, invite vendors to respond to a structured request for proposals.

What Are Best Practices for BI Reports?

Structured, periodic reports remain at the center of data-driven decision support for managerial decision making. The reports may be in portable document format (PDF) and the reports are probably Web accessible, but we still create and use reports. Twenty-five years ago, one would see piles of computer printouts in a manager's office. Today, reports include graphs in color with professional looking tables, but we still print reports. Managers and IS/IT staff need to know how to design reports. Why do we print reports? Managers can quickly scan a paper report while multi-tasking and many managers are reluctant to read reports online.

Many reports are hurriedly constructed, repetitive, and create information overload. Managers think they know what they want in reports and that and more is what they get from an accommodating IS/IT staffer. After all, the IS/IT staffer does not know exactly what information a manager needs, and when, to help manage the business. In addition, most IS/IT staffers have not been taught how to design decision-relevant reports.

IS/IT staff keep hoping reports will "go away" with Web-based end user access to data. What is happening is that some managers and staff are creating reports that must be printed to disseminate them.

Training in report writing in many companies is focused on the technical capabilities of reporting software and report wizards step a manager or staffer "through creating simple reports without writing any code." So most reports are pages after pages of data. Too many fields are often displayed, table headings are cryptic, or names are from the database. Basic context information such as date of the report, who prepared it, and a title that suggests that the purpose of the report is forgotten, and gratuitous charts and cross tabulations are included because it is easy to do so and not because of user needs. Many existing reports slow decision making rather than increase decision-making effectiveness.

Both periodic and ad hoc BI reports may be primarily informational, analytical, or comparative. The informational reports summarize what has happened for a time period and may focus on key performance indicators (KPIs) and critical success factors. Analytical reports do more than summarize; such reports emphasize averages, deviations, trends and cross tabulations. Comparative reports usually focus on internal comparisons such as actual versus budgeted or sales by category compared to a prior quarter or year. Some comparison reports include external data.

Some periodic reports are generated in an operational data-driven DSS automatically. These reports often answer the "what is happening right now?" question. Other periodic and ad hoc reports are intended to answer specific decision-related questions. Predefined reports are usually still developed by the IS/IT department in response to a user request. With easier-to-use report generator tools, many users generate their own reports. Neither IS/IT nor most users do much report planning. The tools make it so fast to get the data into a report that the objectives, purpose, and best design for the specific report are often forgotten.

So what are some "best practices" guidelines for designing reports used to support decision making? We have more guidelines for E-mail and Website usability than we do for BI reports. But managers do not need guideline overload. The following is a short list.

1. Keep reports simple and short! Shorter is better and for performance monitoring a one-page report is ideal. Do not create complex, hard to understand reports.

2. Charts and graphs should add meaning and convey a single message. Just because it is easy to create charts, it does not mean you need them. A chart often conveys a lot of information, but a chart needs annotation, a descriptive title, and labels to be useful.

3. Do not overload the user with too many numbers and too much detail. Providing pages of detailed data is not a report. Some managers want detail in a report. That is usually because they do not trust the accuracy of the summarized data. After a period of time, a manager may gain trust in the data and request more summarization. Then an effective report can be designed.

4. When possible, use color, shading, or graphics such as arrows to highlight key findings, discrepancies, or major indicators. In a paper or Web-based report you should not rely on color alone to convey differences in charts or tables.

5. Create and follow report design guidelines. Educate people who create reports about effective reporting.

6. Talk to managers/users of a periodic report. Discuss report design with the person who requests the report and provide help for people who create ad hoc reports.

7. Make the context and purpose of a report obvious to anyone who sees it. At the beginning of a report, state objectives, authorization, important background facts, and limitations of the data. Always include the date and title on every page of a physical or electronic report. Use page numbers and specify restrictions on distribution and confidentiality.

8. Make a plan for the production and design of the report. Sketch tables and charts and plan the order of information that is included. Decide what data to include and decide how to arrange the detailed data. Make explicit decisions about titles, headings, and data formats.

Information technology staff must work with the managers who will read and use the reports; the problem of bad or ineffective reports is usually "people-related" not "technology-related." Great reports lead to better and faster data-driven decisions.

What Are Examples of Routine Decision Support Queries?

In the mid-1980s, powerful relational database management systems (RDBMS) such as Oracle and IBM DB2 encouraged managers to expect answers directly from a company database. The idea was that managers would write and process their own English-like questions using structured query language (SQL). That hope was not realistic given the technology. Writing even simple queries is challenging and a poorly constructed query can slow other computer processing. SQL, pronounced "see-quel" or "S" "Q" "L," still exists and routine decision support questions are included in decision support applications accessing an RDBMS.

SQL is a nonprocedural, declarative computing language. The person who writes a query in SQL specifies what data they want, but a detailed procedure of how to obtain the result is not specified. The person writing the query must understand the keywords and syntax of SQL to write meaningful questions. The keywords in SQL are English words with similar meanings, but the grammar of queries is much more structured than in English.

Why is it difficult for managers to write their own queries? The structure of tables in a database is closely related to the design of SQL queries. Hence, the first problem for managers is to understand the tables and relationships in the database they want to use. Databases can have many tables. The good news is that tables are reasonably fixed and static and managers may only use a subset of the tables. Having unique field names in the tables can also help. The second problem is actually to write a decision support question as a meaningful structured query.

Let us examine some routine decision support queries that managers might want to execute. Each is a SELECT query, data is selected from the database. In some cases, a query aggregates or summarizes data. What are some routine decision support queries?

Who was the top salesperson last month?
When did salesperson Joe Smith join the organization?
What salespeople have birthdays next month?
Who was our largest customer last month?
How many hours have been devoted to project X in the most recent month?
How many people have worked on the project?
What is the average time spent last week by employees assigned to project X?
What did our largest customer buy?
What products had the largest gains in sales last quarter?
How do last week's sales compare to the prior week's sales?
What was the best selling item last month?
What products are currently out of stock?

BI tools have made it easier to query a relational database without understanding SQL. A graphical interface takes user's question and "writes" and executes the SQL query. Basically, BI tools add a layer on top of SQL to help people write queries. Some managers can work directly with current BI tools, but even the best tools can be challenging to learn and use.

What SQL Knowledge Do Managers Need for Decision Support Queries?

SQL is considered difficult for most managers to learn and use. SQL is a complex language with many capabilities, but some managers can learn to manipulate and retrieve data in a decision support query. Most managers need only limited knowledge of SQL. As noted, a decision support question or query to a database must be structured to conform to the SQL command language rules. The following are some basics.

First, begin all decision support queries with the key word SELECT. This command key word tells the database program that you want to find and retrieve data. You often need to end the query with a semicolon (;).

Second, list the data fields you want to retrieve. If the field name is unique, the name is adequate. If the name is used in multiple tables, then specify the table name and then the field name. If you want multiple fields, then separate the names using commas. The asterisk (*) can be used to retrieve all fields in a table.

Third, if you want only distinct or nonduplicate values from fields, specify the keyword DISTINCT; by default all values, even duplicates, are returned from a query.

Fourth, a query must specify the tables where the data is located. The keyword FROM precedes a list of tables.

Fifth, if only some of the data is relevant or needed, the keyword WHERE is used to limit the dataset for results. Operators including equals (=), greater than (>), BETWEEN, LIKE, and IN are used in the WHERE clause to specify a condition. The logical operators AND and OR filter records based on more than one condition.

Sixth, if data that is retrieved should be arranged in an ascending or descending order, then use the keyword ORDER BY to indicate the field used to order the data and specify ascending or descending.

Seventh, if data in a field needs to be aggregated or summarized, use specialized analytical function keywords including AVG(), SUM(), and COUNT() to create new results.

Eighth, in some situations it is necessary to group and create subsets of data before applying a function. In addition, a query may limit output based on a calculated value. The keywords GROUP BY and HAVING are used in these situations.

Ninth, SQL "joins" are used to query data from two or more tables, based on a relationship between certain columns in these tables. There are a number of ways to specify joining two or more tables. The easiest way to join two tables is to use the WHERE keyword and the equal operator.

Tenth, queries can be complex. It may be necessary to use multiple queries to answer a single decision support question. The result of one query is used by another query and you can include nested queries in WHERE and HAVING clauses. If you need to nest queries to retrieve the desired data, consider asking for help.

What Method Is Best for Building an Enterprise-Wide, Data-Driven Decision Support Application?

Using a methodology similar to the Systems Development Life Cycle (SDLC) provides one way managers and organizations can systematically approach the development of a decision support database and decision support end user capabilities. Once system requirements are fixed, SDLC limits changes and reduces development flexibility. Development of a large, shared enterprise-wide, data-driven DSS is usually an undertaking of great complexity. Organizational decision-making information needs are varied and needs often change in response to problems and new tasks. Some flexibility in the development process is usually needed.

Because of design and development problems, some highly innovative and potentially useful decision support applications have been failures. Often the problem is the system is built from the perspective of the developer. Effective decision support, analytics and BI must be built with extensive user input and feedback.

Gathering and organizing corporate historical data and relevant external data so people can access the data and derived information creates both technical and organizational problems. The method used should help developers resolve both types of problems.

In general, building an enterprise-wide DSS that queries a DW should proceed incrementally, but developers should follow a structured, planned approach. An incremental approach allows builders the opportunity to get feedback on prototypes of capabilities while reducing the risks associated with building an enterprise-wide system.

Inmon[2] suggests creating the overall DW conceptual plan and then implementing the subjects that are most important to stakeholders. His spiral development method is based on incremental commitment.

Follow eight steps to build an enterprise-wide, data-driven DSS.[3]

Step 1: Decision-oriented diagnosis and definition of requirements. What are the current decision processes that need data-driven decision support the most and what are the information needs?

Step 2: Feasibility analysis of a DW and BI decision support system. Do we need and can we afford such a system? Will we benefit?

Step 3: Investigate current data. Examine the enterprise data model if it exists. Identify and describe the structure of data in current operational systems.

Step 4: Create a plan for how historical data is to be organized. This is the process of identifying, modeling, and documenting the data requirements of the system being designed. The data are separated into topics on which managers need information. Then developers define how the topics are related.

Step 5: Create tables and relations, and move data into the tables from operational or external systems.

Step 6: Create demonstration of decision support applications for a few targeted users.

Step 7: Have targeted users test the capabilities and provide feedback.

Step 8: If justified, incrementally expand the decision support project and return to Step 5.

The above steps provide a flexible, "agile" development method without the sharp distinctions of other structured methods such as the Systems Development Life Cycle (SDLC) or Waterfall approach.

Ideally, the above eight-step approach will (a) encourage collaboration and interactions among the development team and potential users and encourage use of processes and tools; (b) ensure that the applications work as intended, but promote adequate documentation; (c) create feedback during development and recognize that ongoing collaboration is important. Intended users, "the customers," should have realistic expectations and an implicit "contract" with the developers. The eight steps provide incremental commitment of resources and provide an open, adaptive development process. Decision support needs and technologies can, and often do, change during a project.

In many situations, a full-scale life cycle development approach is too rigid for building decision support capabilities, especially proposed systems the requirements of which are changing rapidly. Changes in requirements are often expensive, but necessary. For innovative decision support, the development method should not limit change, rather it must accommodate needed change.

Developers and future users need predictability and adaptability when implementing a traditional data-driven DSS. Developers do not need to choose between agile and structured development for decision support.

What Are Sources of Data for Building a Data-Driven DSS?

Managers and IT staff who think about opportunities for building innovative, data-driven DSS should explore this question. Too often it is answered hurriedly and without reflection and the answer given is to use data from transactional systems, accounting systems, or operational data stores. Nevertheless, many other sources, both internal and external to an organization, are possible decision support data sources. In many cases, the internal source data is not being recorded or captured and the external sources may be expensive or require new data collection methods. Despite these difficulties, data-driven DSS should not be built using convenient, easy to use, readily available data, unless the data is useful for meeting a decision support need.

Building a data-driven DSS that only has easily accessible data usually limits the usefulness of the system. Such an approach is reminiscent of the story of a man searching for a lost gold coin on a dark night. A passerby sees the man on his hands and knees searching by a street light and asks if he can help. The searcher says sure and tells him of his lost gold coin. The passerby gets on his knees and starts looking and eventually gets frustrated. He then asks "When and how did you lose this piece of gold?"

The searcher relates he was walking down this sidewalk an hour ago and he dropped the coin accidentally and it rolled. Our patient passerby then asks, "Why are we searching here?" Calmly the man who lost the coin explains, "There is a street light here."

Limiting analysis to easily accessible data is similar to searching under a street light. Just because we have that data and just because it is in a DW does not mean that by using it we can find the answers for our decision support questions. So what sources should managers consider? In addition, if we think a source may be useful, how can we get the data?

Some potential sources of useful decision support data include:

1. *Commercial Data Sources*. Often for a fee, organizations can purchase data on current and potential customers, suppliers, or products. This data may need to be merged and sorted with internal data to make it useful for decision support. Privacy, licensing, and copyright issues need to be evaluated when considering commercial data sources. Much more data will become available from commercial sources in future years, the problem is that competitors can also obtain this data.

2. *Customer/Stakeholder Surveys and Questionnaires*. Many firms will plan and conduct surveys using Web forms, telephone, or mail interview protocols. Randomly offering customers a chance to respond to an automated telephone survey and receive a reward of some type can be a quick, systematic way to gather customer satisfaction data. Similar approaches can be used with employees and other stakeholders.

3. *Direct Observation and Data Capture*. Organization members and paid observers can regularly capture and record data on customer or competitor behaviors of interest to managers. A Web form can record the observations and make the data available for decision support.

4. *Government Data Sources*. Local, state, federal, and international government agencies are major suppliers of data. Finding and organizing the data can be a major task.

5. *Passive Electronic Data Capture*. Radio frequency identifiers, bar code readers, and other data capture technologies can be implemented to

gather innovative data. Privacy concerns may be an issue, but full disclosure and consent forms can help deal with such concerns. Affinity cards for customers or identification badges can be integrated into the data collection system.

6. *Transaction Data.* The record keeping systems in organizations have extensive useful data. In some cases, the systems need to capture additional data at the point of sale or when a transaction occurs to really provide good data for decision support. In addition, transaction systems may have data quality problems that must be corrected.

The colorful term "big data" refers to large sets of structured and unstructured data. Data sets are continually increasing in size and may grow too large for traditional storage and retrieval. Data may be captured and analyzed as and when it is created and then stored in files.

We have too much data and yet not always the right data, that is the good news and the bad news about data sources. We want quality data that is relevant to meeting our decision support needs. For data-driven decision making, explore many potential sources of data when you identify a decision support need, do not get talked into searching under the street light.

What Is ETL Software and How Is It Related to BI and Decision Support?

Data warehousing practitioners experience frustration when creating a large data store from existing operating databases that use a variety of data models and technologies. ETL software attempts to make that task easier. ETL is an acronym for extract, transform, and load. This type of software is also called *data extraction software.*

In managing databases, ETL refers to a software package with three primary functions: EXTRACT reads data from a specified database and writes a subset of data to a file; TRANSFORM changes the new data set using rules or lookup tables; finally, LOAD writes the data set to a database intended to support reporting, queries, drill down, and other decision support solutions.

ETL software can be used to create a temporary data set for a specific decision support purpose or it may be used to create and refresh a more permanent data mart or enterprise data warehouse (EDW).

ETL software is needed because in many situations, the data that managers want to analyze is in diverse databases and in diverse formats. ETL software can get existing data into a form and format that is useful in a specific decision support task. In addition, in some situations ETL software can be used to improve data quality and data integration. According to a Business Objects press release, ETL is "a critical building block to a successful business intelligence deployment."

The ETL task is a complex problem in most companies and for most decision support projects. The goal is to extract comparable data that is consistent and then "clean up" the data and structure it for rapid queries.[4]

So, ETL software helps prepare data from diverse data sources for use in a data-driven DSS. ETL is part of the DW/data-driven DSS development process. ETL software does NOT however ensure the quality of decision support data—it is only a tool that needs to be used intelligently.

How Important Are Pivot Tables in Data-Driven Decision Support?

Some analysis tools are used more and are used more effectively than others. For example, pivot tables have become key analysis tools since Microsoft included the capability with Excel. Companies have massive amounts of information and have difficulty managing, retrieving, and analyzing it.[5] Lohr discusses this problem and asserts that "data-driven decision making" can increase productivity by 5–6 percent. Pivot tables are a key tool for analyzing and summarizing large amounts of data.

A pivot table is a data summarization tool found in many data visualization applications that use data from a spreadsheet/worksheet or database. Pivot tools sort, count, total, or average data stored in a table or spreadsheet. The tool displays the results in a representation called a "pivot table" that shows the summarized data. Pivot tools quickly create cross tabulations. The user sets up and changes the table structure by dragging and dropping fields. This "rotation" or pivoting of the summary table gives the concept its name.

According to MacDonald,[6] a pivot table "tallies key amounts, like the average amount spent for a customer in a specific city, education level, or gender. However, there are several potentially important relationships, and, therefore, several types of summary tables that you could create. Pivot tables are the perfect tool because they give you almost unlimited flexibility when you want to figure out different relationships."

There are three key reasons for organizing data into a pivot table: (a) The pivot table summarizes data into a compact, understandable format; (b) It helps find relationships in data; and (c) It organizes the data in a format that is easy to chart.

Pivot tables are an easy to use and easy to understand analytical tool for managers. Perhaps "data scientists" will use more sophisticated statistical and modeling tools, but keeping the tool simple and easy to use is also important. From that perspective, the pivot table tool is important to data-driven decision support. Simple analytics are often all that we require to get insight from big data sets.

In an analysis, we want to avoid three types of errors. A type I error occurs when we incorrectly reject the null or no relationship hypothesis. Our error is a false positive. A type II error occurs when we accept the no relationship hypothesis when there is in fact a relationship. Our error is a false negative. A type III error occurs when we ask the wrong question. Our error is in accepting an answer that is irrelevant to the problem.

Spreadsheet applications such as Excel are a desktop analysis tool that can be used by an analyst or a manager to summarize data, visualize relationships among variables, and forecast trends. The keys to using a tool such as Excel are:

1. To have a good dataset that you know how to manipulate. Are there missing data values? How many rows of data should be in the dataset?
2. To be familiar with the Excel data analysis tools, especially pivot tables. What is a pivot table? What does it mean to pivot? What is drill down? What is a pivot chart?
3. To know when to use different types of charts. What chart is most appropriate for the analysis? What is a regression line? How do you change titles, data series, chart attributes?

The biggest challenges we encounter in data-driven decision support are (a) gathering accurate, useful data; (b) having the data easily accessible for analysis; (c) asking the right questions of available data; and (d) finally, carrying out the analysis correctly with appropriate tools.

Pivot tables do not solve all of our problems, but they can increase the chances our analysis will be useful and correct.

Is Parallel Database Technology Needed for Data-Driven DSS?

Few managers have heard of parallel computer processing and parallel databases. Nonetheless, the desire of managers for more and better historical data is increasing the need for such capabilities.

Norman and Thanisch[7] with Bloor Research Group argue that the future of commercial databases "is bound up with the ability of databases to exploit hardware platforms that provide multiple CPUs." They also note, "There is a tremendous amount of confusion in the market over parallel database technology, among both customers and the vendors." Because few decision makers have much understanding of parallel databases, they argue "it is open season for database and hardware marketing people to confuse the market with technical mumbo-jumbo, that they don't fully understand themselves." Parallel database technology makes it possible to process very large databases for data-driven decision support.

Parallel processing divides a computing task into smaller tasks that can be processed independently. Hence, the larger task is completed more quickly. Parallel relational database systems store data that is spread across many storage disks and accessed by many processing units. Massively parallel processing "is the coordinated processing of a program by multiple processors that work on different parts of the program, with each processor using its own operating system and memory."[8]

A Teradata Warehouse technical overview[9] has the following example of parallel processing: "Imagine that you were handed a shuffled stack of playing cards and were not allowed to scan the cards beforehand. Then you were asked a simple question, 'How many aces are in the stack?' The only way to get the answer would be to scan the entire deck of cards. Now imagine that the same cards were distributed among four people, each receiving one-fourth of the cards. The time required to answer this same query is now reduced by four times. Each person would simply have to scan their cards, and the four totals would be aggregated for the correct answer. In this simple example, we can refer to these four people as parallelized units of work."

Mahapatra and Mishra[10] provide another example: "Your local grocery store provides a good, real-life analogy to parallel processing. Your grocer must collect money from customers for the groceries they purchase. He could install just one checkout stand, with one cash register, and force everyone to go through the same line. However, the line would move slowly, people would get fidgety, and some would go elsewhere to shop. To speed up the process, your grocer doubtless uses several checkout stands, each with a cash register of its own. This is parallel processing at work. Instead of checking out one customer at a time, your grocer can now handle several at a time."

So imagine many relational databases linked together where each database has the same data organization and queries are simultaneously asked of all the databases and answers from each database are then summarized.

Parallel database technology is critical to the future success of data-driven DSS. According to Todd Walter[11] of Teradata Inc., three issues are driving the increasing use of parallel processing in database environments: (a) the need for increased speed or performance for large databases; (b) the need for scalability; and (c) the need for high availability. In 2000, Mahapatra and Mishra concluded, "Intra-query parallelism is very beneficial in decision support system (DSS) applications, which often have complex, long-running queries. As DSS have become more widely used, database vendors have been increasing their support for intra-query parallelism."

In general, parallel processing is necessary to provide timely results from complex, decision support database queries needed by managers in data intensive organizations.

What Is a Data Warehouse Appliance?

In general, a DW appliance is an integrated hardware and software bundled application. A DW appliance includes server hardware and premium storage technology with an installed operating system, database management system, and application software tuned for data warehousing. Most DW appliances use massively parallel processing architectures to provide fast query performance and platform scalability. Any type of appliance is a purpose-specific device.

A DW appliance can range from a small capacity device to a much more powerful platform for storage and querying. Many argue that Netezza was the first vendor to offer data warehouse appliances. Netezza started operations in the early 2000s. The company was acquired by IBM in 2010. Netezza's appliances use a proprietary Asymmetric Massively Parallel Processing (AMPP) architecture that "combines open, blade-based servers and disk storage with a proprietary data filtering process using field-programmable gate arrays."[12]

In February 2010, Netezza announced that it had opened up its systems to support major programming models, including Hadoop, MapReduce, Java, C++, and Python models.

Netezza's main competitors include Oracle Exadata and Teradata. Oracle Exadata Database Machine (http://www.oracle.com) uses Oracle Exadata Storage Servers that combine smart storage software and industry-standard hardware. Oracle Exadata Storage Servers use a massively parallel architecture to increase data bandwidth between the database server and storage. The Teradata Data Warehouse Appliance (http://www.teradata.com) features the Teradata Database, a Teradata platform with dual quad core processors, the SUSE® Linux operating system, and enterprise-class storage. Other competitors include Microsoft SQL server bundled with HP technology.

DW appliances are cost effective for small, dedicated DW. As DW applications increase, IT managers may be tempted to install multiple DW appliances. This strategy can lead to problems of data duplication and data discrepancies among data marts/warehouses.

What Is Mobile Business Intelligence?

Mobile BI refers to data-driven decision support applications on mobile devices such as smartphones and tablet computers. Mobile BI uses wireless devices to support data transfer and operations decision making. Mobile BI applications exist for Android, Blackberry, iPhone/iPad, and

Windows Mobile operating systems. In general, the phrase refers to a rapidly emerging decision support application area. More applications are becoming available from startups and traditional BI vendors for innovative dashboards, live reports, CRM, and performance monitoring.

Mobile delivery of BI is about providing tactical information needed to make immediate decisions. "People are looking for information to address a particular question or to complete a transaction," says Gartner analyst Ted Friedman. "The biggest value is in operational BI—information in the context of applications—not in pushing lots of data to somebody's phone. What you want to send them is the exceptions, the alerts, or what they really need to act on now."[13]

Samir Sakpal,[14] an analyst at Frost & Sullivan, predicts that mobile analytics will move beyond niche markets, such as the financial sector, into mainstream use because, he says, it helps businesses do two things: "Make faster decisions and drive a higher quality of customer service."

Tablets are an important delivery platform for mobile BI. Tablets are a new computing form factor. In computing, a form factor specifies the physical dimensions of computing platforms and major system components. Common form factors for computing platforms include handheld, tablet, and desktop and enterprise computers. Innovations in the computing form factor have previously resulted in increased penetration of decision support in organizations.

There are many YouTube videos related to mobile BI. For example, there are demonstrations of the PushBI Mobile Business Intelligence solution shown on the Apple iPad device, Oco's mobile SaaS BI solutions, and arcplan Mobile. Umesh Jain argues in Digital Software Magazine, "The mobile BI landscape is still in the early stages of development, with MicroStrategy, QlikView, and Roambi taking the early lead in offering and focus."[15] The tablet form factor creates excitement and new application possibilities for decision support and BI.

Conclusions

We use many different terms for systems labeled data-driven DSS. What is important for managers is understanding the concepts associated with helping people access, analyze, and understand large amounts of complex data. We can call this category of systems and software data-driven DSS, *BI, DW software, analytics, multidimensional analysis software, OLAP, reporting analytics,* or *EIS*.

Data-driven DSS target decision makers who need access to large amounts of business data. These systems have evolved from simple verification of facts to analysis of the data and now to discovery of new relationships in large historical data sets. Data-Driven DSS software products are also evolving to better support this wide range of activities. Managers can verify facts using intuitive, easy to use query and reporting tools. Decisions-makers can conduct analyses using data and statistical tools. In addition, managers and decision support analysts can discover new relationships in data using knowledge discovery and data mining tools.

Data-driven decision support is also evolving in terms of technology and architecture. Organizations deliver decision support capabilities using mobile and World Wide Web technologies to managers located almost anywhere in the world. Mobile decision support is an exciting frontier that is broadening the use of data in decision making.

Data-driven DSS are crucial systems for providing managers with the information they want, when they want it, and in a format that is "decision impelling." When we build a data-driven DSS, we are organizing and summarizing data in multiple dimensions for fast retrieval and for ad hoc analysis. The primary goal of these systems is to help managers transform data into information and knowledge. Real-time operations, management control, and strategic planning activities can be supported.

In conclusion, managers and especially technical managers need a broad foundation of knowledge about BI and data-driven decision support.

Summary

BI and data-driven DSS refer to computerized systems to help managers get facts from historical data. Some authors include data mining as data-driven DSS, but data mining is a type of special study. Data warehousing refers to the process of collecting, organizing, and managing historical data in a database. The amount of data stored is increasing in amount and variety. Organizations now have access to "big data" stores.

Some data stores include external data for comparison reports and organizations continue to increase the amount and type of data captured and stored including web traffic and social media data. Developers and managers need to jointly determine sources of data for decision support data stores. In addition to company data, there are commercial data sources, government sources, and innovative data capture from passive and social media sources.

Parallel database technology is increasingly important for data-driven decision support using "big data." DW appliances are cost effective for small, dedicated DW. Data-driven DSS are important for decision makers who need access to and summary of large amounts of business-relevant data.

Mobile delivery of decision support and BI provides tactical information needed to make immediate decisions.

CHAPTER 5

Predictive Analytics and Model-Driven Decision Support

Companies are implementing predictive analytics and quantitative models to assist managers. There remain, however, important knowledge gaps about how to implement analytics and especially predictive analytics and model-driven decision support. In general, analytics refers to quantitative analysis of data. Analytics may be part of a data-driven or a model-driven DSS. Predictive analytics is about using models for predicting behavior or results. Predictive analytics can help managers make choices and develop competitive actions.

Many banks use analytics and model-driven DSS when making credit and lending decisions. Trucking and delivery firms use quantitative models to generate optimal routes and fueling stop recommendations. Police Departments use predictive analytics software to better allocate resources and identify crime patterns to prevent crime and increase public safety. Managers use model-driven DSS to establish pricing for customers. Companies use Web-based systems for planning, budgeting, reporting, and analysis. Factory managers and staff use optimization tools to balance manufacturing constraints while achieving more production output. A number of railroad companies use decision support systems for train dispatching and yard management.

According to Davenport, Cohen, and Jacobson,[1] companies "use analytical tools to change the way they compete or to perform substantially better in the existing business model." They argue that gaming firm Harrah's competes on analytics "for customer loyalty and service, rather than on building the mega-casinos in which its competitors have invested." They note Amazon.com uses extensive analytics to predict successful products.

Sales forecasting software uses a moving average or econometric model; trending analytics improve fleet management profit-and-loss factors such as fuel consumption and safety performance; representational DSS use simulation models; and optimization DSS generate optimal solutions consistent with constraints and assist in scheduling and resource allocation. Model-driven DSS assist in forecasting product demand, aid in employee scheduling, develop pro forma financial statements, or assist in choosing plant or warehouse locations. Model-driven DSS are developed for various purposes using a variety of quantitative and statistical techniques.

Model-driven decision support provides managers with models and analysis capabilities to use during the process of making a decision. The range and scope of model-driven DSS is very broad. New commercial products are regularly announced, Web-based applications are widely deployed, mobile applications are increasingly common, and companies develop their own proprietary systems. To exploit opportunities for this type of support, DSS analysts and managers need to understand analytical tools and modeling. Building some categories of models requires considerable expertise. Many specialized books discuss and explain how to implement simulation and mathematical programming models. Companies use both custom and off-the-shelf model-driven decision support applications.

Nine questions associated with predictive analytics and model-driven decision support are answered in the remaining sections of this chapter.

What Are Analytic Applications?

Henry Morris, senior vice president for IDC's Worldwide Software and Services research group, claims he coined the term *analytic applications* in 1997. In an article titled "Trends in Analytic Applications," Morris argued that an analytic application must meet each of the following three conditions: (a) provide process support—it structures and automates a group of tasks pertaining to the review and optimization of business operations or the discovery and development of new business; (b) have separation of function—"the application can function independently of an organization's core transactional applications, yet it can be dependent on such applications for data and might send results back to these applications"; and (c) use time-oriented, integrated data from multiple sources.[2]

According to Morris in the same article, analytic applications in three areas meet the above criteria: (a) financial/business performance management; (b) operations/production; and (c) customer relationship management (CRM). He notes that for an analytical application, technical specialists build the model using sophisticated tools. Decision makers then apply the model, gauging the probable impact of a planned course of action. Morris notes, "analytic applications will co-exist with business intelligence tools."

We have been building analytic applications and conducting analyses for a long time. The term *analytic application* refers to a broad generic set of information systems that are generally model-driven decision support applications. In Morris' taxonomy, DSS that emphasize unplanned or ad hoc user inquiries are not analytic applications, rather he classifies them as BI applications.

Gemignani, in an informative blog post about why analytical applications fail, asserts that applications "fail for a simple reason: they assume users know precisely what they need before they've begun the analysis."[3] Designers need to avoid this assumption. Analytical applications should let users "play" with the results and test various assumptions and change parameters.

What Is Analytical Processing?

Transforming data and then summarizing it is a key task in many decision-making situations. Once this task is complete, a manager analyzes and then tries to understand the information created. Analytical processing involves performing quantitative data transformations and mathematical and statistical summarization and generating decision-relevant results. Processing refers to obtaining data and performing the quantitative operations on the data. Analytical processing occurs in data and model-driven DSS and in special decision support studies.

The term *online analytical processing* (OLAP) was introduced in 1993 by Dr E.F. Codd.[4] It refers to software used to manipulate multi-dimensional data from a variety of sources that has been stored in a data warehouse. Analytical processing software helps users create various views and representations of data. OLAP software provides fast, consistent, and interactive access to shared, multidimensional data.[5] OLAP, as part of a data-driven DSS, is used to discover trends and perform statistical analyses. Reporting analytics based on OLAP differ from predictive analytics. Reporting analytics are used for business intelligence.

Examples of analytical operations used in model and data-driven DSS and in special studies include (a) cross tabulation; (b) summarizations such as average, range, and sum; (c) clustering; (d) regression; (e) goal seeking; (f) multivariable analyses (multiple scenarios); and (g) calculations of percentages, deviations, and differences.

Cross tabulation creates a two-dimensional table showing the interaction of two variables. This type of analytical operation is easy to understand and is commonly implemented as a pivot table to provide easy changes in analysis. A pivot table is an interactive data summarization tool.

Clustering assigns data into subsets based on a criterion and distance measure. Clusters of data observations are hence similar in some way (e.g., frequent buyers vs. infrequent buyers).

Regression is a statistical tool for analyzing relationships among data. The model has a data variable (dependent variable) that is determined or predicted by one or more other variables (independent variables). The most common type of regression is simple, linear regression. This technique assumes a straight line, linear relationship between a dependent variable and a single independent variable. Regression is often used for prediction.

More complex algebraic, mathematical programming and simulation models are used in model-driven DSS. In addition, data-driven DSS often use analytical tools such as pivot tables, drill down, and dashboard displays. Special studies use a wide variety of quantitative and analysis tools. The analytical processing is often ad hoc and conducted by a human analyst preparing the study.

Much of computerized decision support is about providing managers with predetermined analyses. In some systems, managers have limited capabilities to change the analysis and other systems provide extensive "what if?" capabilities. Analytical processing is a fundamental capability associated with computerized decision support.

How Does Predictive Analytics Support Decision Making?

Predictive analytics refers to using models to support forecasting, planning, and operational decision making. Data is analyzed to build a predictive model to support a specific decision task. The decision task may be determining who to target in a marketing campaign, what products to stock, detect the possibility of fraud, or determine who the "best" customers are for a firm. Using historical data, predictor variables are identified for quantitative or business rule models. The model makes a prediction related to a decision task.

Managers in consumer packaged goods, retail, banking, gambling, energy, and healthcare industries are the most active users of predictive analytics. Predictive analytics are increasingly incorporated in day-to-day operations management tasks using real-time or near real-time systems. New projects can be implemented faster because software has improved for analysis and development, but the number of IT professionals skilled in using the many varied analytical techniques is inadequate to meet the demand for new capabilities.

Developing predictive analytics should involve both business and IT managers. This joint development process helps in understanding and in some cases automating business operational decisions. Meaningful collaboration between managers and technical specialists facilitates improved and enhanced routine decision making. Analytics development can serve as a bridge between IT and business stakeholders.

Predictive analytics are increasingly important in large and medium-sized organizations. Development and use of predictive analytics should be a core technology competency of many companies and managers should be reluctant to outsource or offshore the capability. Managers must realize that the cost of each analytics project is an investment in building competency and it can also reduce operations costs and enhance operations. There is a learning curve associated with building predictive models and analyzing data, but consultants can reduce the curve. Managers should not, however, assume that developers outside their firm can easily understand the peculiarities and needs of their business. As organizations capture more data, it will be important to analyze and use the data to enhance business results.

Predictive analytics is one tool in the broad field of decision support. Based on various sources and especially the IBM Analytics Quotient (AQ) quiz,[6] the following questions and answers provide "best practice" advice for using IT to implement analytics including predictive analytics. These practices are also relevant to developing data-driven decision support (see discussion of data sources in Chapter 4).

1. What types of data sources should managers and staff analyze as part of decision making?

   Answer: In general, data sources from all organization functions should be combined with data from text sources, point of sale, RFID, commercial data sources, and social media.

2. How important is the quality of data used in analyses?

   Answer: **Data quality is very important.** An organization should have an enterprise data model. Metadata is very important and strong data governance practices must be in place.

3. Should managers document outcomes of analytics initiatives?

   Answer: **Yes, documentation is important.** Managers should initiate a documentation process to capture how business analytics changes business operations. Successful projects lead to more projects.

4. How important is using predictive models?

   Answer: **Prediction is very important in operational decision making.** Integrating planning and predictive modeling can enable an organization to adjust policy and execute faster in response to changes in the organization and business environment.

5. Should managers centralize resources for performing and developing analytics?

   Answer: **Yes, but** analytics knowledge should be widespread throughout an organization. Using analytics should become part of the organizational culture. Managers should establish an analytics center of excellence and cross functional analytics teams similar to Six Sigma teams.

6. What general analytics solutions should be implemented in organizations?

   Answer: Solutions are in four categories: (a) Reporting and analytics; (b) Planning, budgeting, and forecasting; (c) Predictive and advanced analytics; and (d) Governance, risk, and compliance.

7. How should managers anticipate future events and results?

Answer: It is important to use both qualitative and quantitative methods, including (a) experience and intuition; (b) predictive analytics for priority needs; (c) "What if" scenarios; and (d) Integrated planning and predictive models.

"Analytics: The Widening Divide" report,[7] a joint MIT Sloan Management Review and IBM Institute of Business Value analytics research partnership, identified three core competencies organizations must master to achieve a competitive advantage with analytics. The first is information management, which focuses on standardized data practices. The second is analytics skills, which revolve on core discipline expertise built on robust tools. Finally, there's a data-oriented culture that sees analytics as a key asset to drive evidence-based management.

Davenport, Cohen, and Jacobsen[8] note, "Instead of competing on traditional factors, companies are beginning to employ statistical and quantitative analysis and predictive modeling as primary elements of competition. These firms have overcome the historical barriers to gathering and managing transaction data and some of the cultural resistance in organizations accustomed to 'gut-feel' decision making, and are using complex analysis and data-intensive decisions to change the way they manage themselves and compete in the marketplace."

Predictive analytics are important decision support tools that lead to fact-based decision making.

What Is a Spreadsheet-Based DSS?

Most managers are familiar with spreadsheet packages such as Microsoft Excel. If a DSS has been or will be implemented using a spreadsheet package, it can be termed a *spreadsheet-based DSS*. The spreadsheet package is the enabling technology for the DSS. Both model-driven and small-scale, data-driven DSS can be implemented using desktop, client-server, or cloud-based spreadsheet applications. Spreadsheet-based DSS can be very useful, but such systems often have errors, are inadequately documented, and are often inappropriate. In addition, spreadsheets are used for special study analytics.

In the world of accounting, a spreadsheet spreads or shows all of the costs, income, taxes, and other financial data on a single sheet of paper for a manager to look at when making a decision. In addition, a spreadsheet is a collection of cells the values of which can be displayed on a computer screen. An electronic spreadsheet organizes data into columns and rows. The data can then be manipulated by a formula to give an average, maximum, or sum. By changing cell definitions and having all cell values reevaluated, a user performs a "what if?" analysis and observes the effects of those changes.[9]

Spreadsheet packages are DSS generators. Sprague and Carlson[10] defined a DSS generator as a computer software package that provides tools and capabilities that help a developer quickly and easily build a specific decision support system. Spreadsheet packages qualify as DSS generators because (a) they have sophisticated data handling and graphic capabilities; (b) they can be used for "what if?" analysis; and (c) spreadsheet software can facilitate the building of a DSS.

Both small-scale, single-user, model-driven and data-driven DSS can be developed using a spreadsheet package. Spreadsheets seem especially appropriate for building DSS with low complexity quantitative models or with small data sets and simple analytics. A developer adds user interface capabilities such as buttons, spinners, and other tools to support a decision maker in "what if?" and sensitivity analyses. For a data-driven DSS, the data set is downloaded to the application from a DBMS, a Website, or a delimited flat file. Then pivot tables and charts help a decision maker summarize and manipulate the data.

Spreadsheet-based DSS can be created in a single-user or a multiuser development environment. Microsoft Excel is certainly the most popular spreadsheet application development environment. Add-in packages such as Crystal Ball, Premium Solver, and @Risk increase the capabilities of a spreadsheet and the variety of models that can be implemented. DSS-Resources.COM has spreadsheet-based DSS case examples from Decisioneering and from Palisade.[11]

Spreadsheet-based DSS do create problems. Business Intelligence vendors and various commentators have pointed out serious problems with documentation and accuracy with the use of spreadsheets.[12] In recent years, reliance on spreadsheet-based DSS has declined as companies implemented enterprise business intelligence systems for decision support. Spreadsheets can satisfy many needs in small, stable organizations, but spreadsheets can become a major burden for managers in larger companies. Managers and IT specialists need to select the right tool for a specific decision support task.

Is ETL Software Needed to Build a Model-Driven DSS?

Extract, transform, and load (ETL) tasks are part of building many types of DSS, including some model-driven DSS. ETL software developed for creating and refreshing large data stores is not needed for model-driven DSS. Model-driven DSS data sets are usually small, and certainly much smaller than the 500 MB—10TB data stores common with the data-driven DSS discussed in Chapter 4.

In some model-driven DSS, the user enters the data needed by the system. The DSS performs data validation and data storage. The data entry may be 5–15 parameter values, text, or other inputs. No data is imported from a source system. For example, the model-driven decision aids at DSSResources.COM have users input the data required by the model.

In other model-driven DSS, a time series of data for one or more variables is imported into the application. The data set may be 1000 to even 10,000 values. It is common to perform extract and transform tasks to create this data set. A data set is exported from a source system. Then because the data set is small the data is usually cleaned up and formatted in a text editor or in a desktop application such as Excel. Excel is often a useful tool for creating small data sets for use with a model-driven DSS. The data set can then be incorporated into a spreadsheet-based DSS or imported into another DSS development environment.

Larger data sets are used for some specialized model-driven DSS, but the size of the data set remains modest compared to the amount of data stored in data marts and data warehouses.

Another common type of model-driven DSS uses a small number of data values from an external database. The user defines the analysis and inputs some parameter values. For example, model-driven investment

DSS extract data from an historical stock market database. The Intrinsic Value per Share Calculator at Quicken.com extracts earnings and price information from a general purpose database of stock information and the user inputs assumptions about interest rates for "What if?" analysis.

Finally, some model-driven DSS use very large data sets to create a visual simulation that the DSS user interacts with. These data sets are created and data may be imported from video files, maps, and other sources. For example, DaimlerChrysler has a Virtual Reality Center to analyze and understand digital models and simulation results. In general, extract, transform, and load tasks for use with quantitative models differ from those associated with data warehousing, business intelligence, and data-driven DSS.

As the data needs of a model(s) in a model-driven DSS increases, it becomes more likely that specialized software will be needed to help the developer create the specific decision support data store. The software used to extract, transform, and load the data depends on the data, the DSS development environment, and the preferences of the developer.

How Does Sensitivity Analysis Differ from "What If?" Analysis?

In the early days of decision support systems, one of the major DSS "selling points" of vendors and academics was the ability to do "What If?" analysis. In the 1970s, a model-driven DSS for sales and production planning allowed a manager to change a decision variable such as the number of units to produce and then immediately get a new result for an outcome variable such as profit. As DSS have gotten more sophisticated and become more diverse, the use of "What If?" as a concept has broadened. We have also introduced more precise terminology from the mathematical modeling literature into our discussions such as the term *sensitivity analysis*.

In most DSS, sensitivity and "What If?" analyses refer to quantitative analyses. In the context of BI and data-driven DSS, "What If?" sometimes refers to ad hoc queries of a decision support database. Planners use models to address "What If" questions such as (a) what profits can we anticipate next year if inflation is 7% and we continue current pricing policies? (b) If we open a new plant, what profits can we expect? (c) What if we were to hire XX people in Sales, XX in Marketing, and XX in R&D next year? (d) What is the impact on manufacturing and shipping costs if the price of oil increases 15% during Q2? and (e) How much raw material inventory is needed if the demand of a product increases 20%?

In the DSS literature and in common discourse, we do not have agreement about the difference between "What If?" analysis and sensitivity analysis. Microsoft Excel 2002 help[13] defines "What-if analysis" as a "process of changing the values in cells to see how those changes affect the outcome of formulas on the worksheet. For example, varying the interest rate that is used in an amortization table to determine the amount of the payments." Four tools in Excel are commonly categorized as "What If?" or sensitivity analysis[14] tools: Data Tables, Goal Seek, Scenarios, and Solver. The simplest type of "What If?" analysis is manually changing a value in a cell that is used in a formula to see the result. Excel experts use the terms sensitivity and "What If?" analyses interchangeably.

To get a better understanding of "What If?" or sensitivity analysis, let us consider MS Excel tools. A data table is a range of cells that summarizes the results of changing certain values in formulas in a model. There are two types of data tables: one-input-variable tables and two-input-variable tables. "Two-variable data tables use only one formula with two lists of input values. The formula must refer to two different input cells." In Microsoft's Mortgage Loan Analysis example, a two-variable data table would show how different interest rates and loan terms would affect the mortgage payment amount. The table shows the decision maker how sensitive the payment amount is to the interest rate.

The Goal Seek tool is helpful when you know the desired result from a model and want to find the appropriate input or decision variable levels. "What If?" involves changing an input until the goal is reached. Goal Seek automates this trial and error process. Scenarios help a user construct strategies where multiple decision variables are changed in each scenario. For example, a decision maker may have best case, most likely, and worst case scenarios. Finally, Solver is an optimization tool that includes a sensitivity analysis capability. Monte Carlo simulation in Excel can also be used to assist in "What If?" or sensitivity analysis. Spreadsheets models with probability distributions for inputs can simulate outcomes for a range of input parameters.

In general, mathematical methods assess the sensitivity of a model's output for a range of values on one or more inputs. Sensitivity analysis is used to determine what inputs, parameters, or decision variables contribute more to the variance in the output of a model and hence what variables are the most important and most "sensitive."

Pannell[15] identifies uses of sensitivity analysis in decision making and in model development. On the basis of his discussion, a model-driven DSS with appropriate sensitivity analysis should help (a) test the robustness of an optimal solution; (b) identify critical values, thresholds, or break-even values where the optimal strategy changes; (c) identify sensitive or important variables; (d) investigate suboptimal solutions; (e) develop flexible recommendations that depend on circumstances; (f) compare the values of simple and complex decision strategies; and (g) assess the "riskiness" of a strategy or scenario.

The most common "What If?" analysis in model-driven DSS is changing an input value in an ad hoc way and seeing the result. This type of analysis has limitations. The analysis is likely to be more complete if an input object such as a spinner or a slider is used to change values. Such an approach is much faster and easier than inputting each new value. A range sensitivity analysis evaluates the effect on outputs by systematically varying one of the model inputs across its entire range of plausible values.

What are the limitations of "What If?" analysis? If the analysis is ad hoc rather than systematic, the analysis is likely to miss potential problems and solutions. Managers may not understand the assumptions of the sensitivity analysis, for example, assuming a linear relationship. In addition, in general, it is impossible to audit the thoroughness of sensitivity and "What If?" analyses and their impact on decision making. Systematic sensitivity analysis using a one or two-variable data table is important in a model-driven DSS based on an algebraic model. Relying on ad hoc manipulation of a single variable in a quantitative model is always problematic and limited.

"What If?" analysis is used broadly for techniques that help decision makers assess the consequences of changes in models and situations. Sensitivity analysis is a more specific and technical term generally used for assessing the systematic results obtained from changing input variables across a reasonable range in a model. The current frontier is animated sensitivity analysis where a visual display such as a chart or graph is systematically varied showing results of changing model parameters.

How Can Simulation Be Used for Decision Support?

Simulation is a broad term that refers to an approach for imitating the behavior of an actual or anticipated human or physical system. The terms *simulation* and *model*, especially quantitative and behavioral models, are closely linked. A model shows the relationships and attributes of interest in the system under study. A quantitative or behavioral model is by design a simplified view of some of the objects in a system. A model used in a simulation can capture more detail about a specific system, but how complex the model is or should be depends on the purpose of the simulation that will be "run" using the model. With a simulation study and when simulation provides the functionality for a DSS, multiple tests, experiments, or "runs" of the simulation are conducted, the results of each test are recorded and then the aggregate results of the tests are analyzed to try to answer specific questions. In a simulation, the decision variables in the model are the inputs that are manipulated in the tests.

In a decision support context, simulation generally refers to a technique for conducting experiments with a computer-based model. One method of simulating a system involves identifying the various states of a system and then modifying those states by setting parameters for specific events. A wide variety of problems can be evaluated using simulation including inventory control and stock-out, manpower planning and assignment, queuing and congestion, reliability and replacement policy, and sequencing and scheduling.

There are several types of simulation models and a variety of terms are used to identify them. These types include Monte Carlo simulation, traditional mathematical simulation, activity-scanning simulation, event-driven simulation, probabilistic simulation, process-based model simulation, real-time simulation, data-driven simulation, agent-based and multiagent simulation, time-dependent simulation, and visual simulation.[16]

In a Monte Carlo or probabilistic simulation, one or more of the independent variables is specified as a probability distribution of values. A probabilistic simulation helps examine risk and uncertainty in a system. Time-dependent or discrete simulation refers to a situation where it is important to know exactly when an event occurs. For example, in waiting lines or queuing problems, it is important to know the precise time of arrival to determine if a customer will have to wait or not. According to Evans and Olson[17] and others, activity-scanning simulation models involve describing activities that occur during a fixed interval of time and then simulating for multiple future periods the consequences of the activities, while process-driven simulation focuses on modeling a logical sequence of events rather than activities. An event-driven simulation also identifies "events" that occur in a system, but the focus is on a time ordering of the events rather than a causal or logical ordering.

Simulation can assist in either a static or a dynamic analysis of a system. A dynamic analysis is enhanced with software that shows the time-sequenced operation of the system that is being predicted or analyzed. Simulation is a descriptive tool that can be used for both prediction and exploration of the behavior of a specific system. A complex simulation can help a decision maker plan activities, anticipate the effects of specific resource allocations, and assess the consequences of actions and events.

In many situations, simulation specialists build a simulation and then conduct a special study analysis and report their results to management. Evans and Olson[18] discuss examples of how simulation has been used to support business and engineering decision making. They report a number of special decision support studies including evaluating the number of hotel reservations to accept to effectively utilize capacity to create an overbooking policy,[19] a Call Center staffing capacity analysis,[20] a study comparing new incinerating system options for a municipal garbage recycling center,[21] a study evaluating government policy options, and various studies for designing facilities. Examples of model-driven DSS built with a simulation as the dominant component include: a Monte Carlo simulation to manage foreign-exchange risks; a spreadsheet-based DSS for assessing the risk of commercial loans; a DSS for developing a weekly production schedule for hundreds of products at multiple plants; a program for estimating returns for fixed-income securities; and a simulation program for setting bids for competitive lease sales.

Agent-based or multiagent simulation does not replace any of the traditional simulation techniques. But in recent years, agent-based visual simulations have become an alternative approach for analyzing some business systems. According to Bonabeau, "People have been thinking in terms of agent-based modeling for many years but just didn't have the computing power to actually make it useful until recently. With agent-based modeling, you describe a system from the bottom up, from the point of view of its constituent units, as opposed to a top-down description, where you look at properties at the aggregate level without worrying about the system's constituent elements."[22]

Agent-based simulations can be used to simulate some natural and man-created systems that cannot be simulated with traditional simulation techniques. Examples of such systems include shoppers in a grocery store, passengers, visitors and employees at an airport, or production workers and supervisors at a factory. The objective of an agent-based simulation is to find a solution that works in the "real world."

A simulation study can answer questions such as how many teller stations will provide 90% confidence that no one will need to wait in line for more than 5 minutes or how likely is it that a specific project will be completed on time and within budget? With a visual simulation decision makers or analysts can observe an airplane in a wind tunnel, a proposed factory in operation, or customers entering a new bank, or a construction project as "it will occur."

Simulation has been used much more for one-time, special decision support studies than it has been used as the model-component in building a model-driven DSS. This is changing with the increased ease in creating visual simulations. Visual simulation means managers can see a graphic display of simulation activities, events and results. Will Wright's games[23] "The Sims," "SimCoaster," and "SimCity" are the precursors for advanced, agent-based, model-driven DSS. Current technologies can support development of complex, faster than real-time, dynamic, agent-based, model-driven DSS for a wide variety of specific decision situations.

Can Multi-User Visual Simulations Provide Real World Decision Support?

Computing technology for creating realistic, multiuser, visual simulations has improved tremendously in the last 25 years. Today, Internet-based multiuser visual simulations are creating excitement and interest in the possibilities of virtual reality for entertainment, e-business, and education. The possibilities for decision support are especially exciting.

Wade Roush, in a 2007 featured article titled "Second Earth" in Technology Review published by MIT,[24] suggests that we will see an even better immersive three-dimensional visual environment that combines a social virtual world such as Second Life with tools such as Google Earth to create a realistic duplicate of our earth.

Roush traces the Metaverse concept to Neil Stephenson's 1992 novel *Snow Crash*.[25] Metaverse was a virtual city. He also notes Yale scientist David Gelernter coined the term *mirror world* to describe accurate simulations of real environments. Roush suggests some decision support applications in mirror worlds or a metaverse that we will summarize as we discuss various types of decision support using realistic simulations.

Chesher[26] notes that "On June 7, 1989 the computer-aided design software company Autodesk and the eclectic computer company VPL announced a new technology called 'virtual reality.'" Virtual reality (VR) is an additional reality, while a mirror world is an extension of reality. Chesher traces the roots of virtual reality to William Gibson's 1984 novel *Neuromancer*.

Movies such as "The Matrix" (1999) and "The Thirteenth Floor" (1999) also deal with the topic of simulated worlds. In "The Matrix," people are connected using cybernetic implants to a simulated reality created by sentient machines to pacify, subdue, and make use of them. In "The Thirteenth Floor," computer scientist Hannon Fuller creates a simulated parallel world with avatars, but the experience is much more immersive.

Daniel F. Galouye's novel *Simulacron-3*[27] also deals with simulated reality. Galouye's novel is the basis for Joseph Rusnal's movie "The Thirteenth Floor." Galouye imagined a simulectronic world that depends "on the Gestalt principle for its verisimilitude—the presence of a sufficient number of items in a pattern to suggest the entire pattern. The cognitive whole is greater than the sum of its perceptible parts."[28]

Envisioning the future has always been a goal of computerized decision support. The environment simulator in *Simulacron-3* was intended to provide probability-based forecasting. The simulator would answer any question about the behavioral and social reactions of people in the simulation. In a special study in a simulated world, avatars can be hired to shop in a newly designed store or to "try and evaluate" a new product before it is produced. Managers can manipulate visual models to try to improve productivity and can interact with a simulated environment before they encounter a similar situation in real life. During the last 15 years, a major application of virtual reality systems has been training for real-life activities. Games such as "Roller Coaster Tycoon" suggest that both avatars and robots can be used in model-driven decision support simulations.

The metaverse, virtual reality, or the simulacron is more than an entertainment technology. Realistic simulation can be a powerful technology for computerized decision support. In 1991, Jaron Lanier[29] argued, "virtual reality is the first medium to come along which doesn't narrow the human spirit..." He said virtual reality would free the imagination of the masses and "help people to communicate" and bring a new kind of spiritual understanding. In a September 1988 white paper[30] titled "Through the Looking Glass," Autodesk founder John Walker argued that virtual reality was the conclusion for improving human–computer interaction.

What Are the Rules for Building a Successful Model-Driven DSS?

In broad terms, to build a successful model-driven decision support application one should strive to (a) identify an influential project champion; (b) prepare for technology shortfalls; (c) tell everyone as much as he or she can about the costs of creating and using the proposed DSS; (d) invest in training; and (e) market and promote the new DSS.

In a 1978 book, Andrew McCosh and Michael Scott Morton[31] discussed some rules for building successful model-based DSS. The conceptual material still seems useful and relevant. They prescribe, "The first rule is keep it simple. Attempts to handle problems which are outside the experience of the people involved are bound to fail no matter what expertise they bring to bear on them. Attempts to jump immediately from a very straight forward procedure ... to a computer-based solution which deals completely with all aspects of the solution are equally pre-doomed." Next they recommend tackling significant problems.

McCosh and Scott Morton focused on model-driven DSS and their rules demonstrate the tension between three groups: (a) decision support theorists, (b) Operations Research specialists, and (c) Information Technology professionals. They argue in rules 3 and 4, "don't let the computer people design the model" and "don't let the operations research staff design the model." McCosh and Scott Morton's rule 5 states, "the manager who is responsible for the subject should be the person who designs the model in its gross form using such help and specialist guidance as he needs."

Managers must have a sense of ownership of any analytic or decision support application and especially applications with a prescriptive model. Decision support designers, whether they have been primarily trained in operations research/management science, computer science or software engineering, need to understand and involve the targeted users of the proposed system in its design.

Rule 6 states "use the staff people to make the model, interacting continuously with the manager as they go." Rule 7 is "test the model and adjust it." Finally, rule 8 is a corollary of rule 1. McCosh and Scott Morton note "while initial simplicity is essential, it also implies that the manager will, with experience, want more complex models built." According to rule 8, "regard the replacement of models by better ones as evidence of vitality, not of earlier errors." After almost 30 years of DSS development, many simple models have probably been replaced. Reviewing McCosh and Scott Morton's rules is informative, but the following simple set of rules provides more contemporary guidance:

Rule 1: *Novel, innovative analytics and model-driven decision support should be initiated by the managers who would use them.*

Rule 2: *Users and technical specialists should periodically review, evaluate, and revise or replace existing model-driven decision support.*

Rule 3: *Decision support and predictive analytics projects must meet a need and provide benefits that justify the ongoing cost of operating, maintaining, and upgrading as well as the cost of building them.*

Rule 4: *Predictive analytics and model-driven systems should be built by teams that include potential users and technical specialists.*

Conclusions

Learning to build models, develop analytics and model-driven DSS is a complex task that requires extensive preparatory work. MIS professionals who want to build models need a strong background in statistics, management science, and operations research. If managers and MIS professionals want to design and build successful model-driven DSS and analytic data-driven systems, they need to expand their skills.

Models are very important components in many DSS, but "bad" models result in "bad" decisions. Many models can be implemented quickly using prototyping. Using prototyping, a new DSS can be constructed in a short time, tested, and improved in several iterations. This development approach helps us test the effectiveness of the overall design. The downside of prototyping is that a new DSS may be hard to deploy to a wide group of users. Managers and decision support analysts need to make sure the scaled down DSS will work when it is deployed more widely in a company.

Many model-driven DSS can be built which use a variety of organizational and external data sets. Managers should be consumers and developers of model-driven DSS. Widely used model-driven DSS need to be built systematically by a team of model specialists, MIS, and network specialists and managers. Small-scale systems can be purchased or built using tools such as Microsoft Excel. New model-driven DSS must capture the complexity of a decision and be easily implemented and integrated into existing systems.

Model-driven DSS remain important support tools for managers, but organizations need to update existing model-based systems and develop new capabilities that can be implemented using Web, visual simulation, and mobile technologies. The current development environments for building model-driven DSS are powerful.

Historically, a small number of experts in statistics, management science, and operations research have performed sophisticated model-driven analyses for companies. As the emphasis on flexibility and competition increases, more and more individuals within companies will need to build and use model-driven DSS. Managers and DSS analysts need to be actively involved in identifying the need for and purpose of model-driven DSS. The capabilities are now more widespread and competition among firms for better decision support has intensified. The demand for more and better analysis is accelerating.

Summary

Many organizations use analytics and model-driven decision support when making important operational decisions. Analytical processing occurs in both data and model-driven DSS and in special decision support studies. Complex algebraic, mathematical programming and simulation models are used in model-driven DSS. In addition, predictive analytics embedded in other information systems support decision making. Historical data is analyzed to build a predictive model to support a specific decision task.

Spreadsheet packages can be used to develop small scale model-driven DSS and to conduct ad hoc analyses. Model-driven and data-driven DSS are the most common types of DSS one would consider developing using a spreadsheet package.

In some model-driven DSS, the user enters the data needed by the system. The DSS performs data validation and data storage. As the data needs of models in a model-driven DSS increases, it becomes more likely that specialized software will be needed to help the DSS developer create the specific decision support data store.

Simulation is increasingly important and developers may use many types of simulation including Monte Carlo, agent-based and multiagent simulation, and visual simulation. Simulation experts should be consulted to help build innovative model-driven support. The basic rule for building successful model-driven decision support is, "decision support projects must meet a need and provide benefits that justify the ongoing cost of operating, maintaining, and upgrading the system as well as the cost of building them".

Models are important for decision support and prediction, but "bad" models result in "bad" decisions. Managers should be intelligent consumers and developers of model-driven DSS and predictive analytics. Quantitative models can assist in making decisions.

CHAPTER 6

Decision Support Benefits and Trade-Offs

Currently, many companies have isolated decision support capabilities that are hard to use or hard to access when needed. For example, a data mart may exist for accessing customer data, a project management system may exist for tracking large-scale projects, and a spreadsheet tool helps in a specific business decision process. Managers have extensive technology possibilities and are experiencing information overload. Creating more information sources is not our goal. Managers need improved and better integrated DSS. Potentially, innovative decision support systems can yield competitive advantage for an organization or at least help maintain an organization's competitive position.

This chapter reviews the benefits of computerized decision support and discusses vendor claims that some systems can create competitive advantage. Research and case studies establish positive results from DSS, but achieving benefits requires a good design and good implementation. An important category of trade-offs involves substitutes for computerized support. The final section examines disadvantages of DSS. Managers need to explore all the trade-offs to improve decision making. Comparing one computerized solution to another ignores the possibilities of changing the decision process.

What Are Potential Benefits of Decision Support?

Evidence indicates that managers can obtain information buried for many years in filing cabinets or archived on computer storage systems by using sophisticated data-driven and document-driven DSS. Model-driven DSS can reduce waste in production operations and improve inventory management. Knowledge-driven DSS can help managers evaluate employees or help technical staff diagnose problems. Communications-driven DSS can support teams working all over the world. DSS can support suppliers and customers with relevant BI. Real-time decision support including predictive analytics can provide tactical decision support.

There are many potential benefits and advantages of implementing computerized decision support capabilities in an organization. Every decision support application will not result in every benefit; and in the worst case, a poorly designed DSS may result in no benefits. Managers need to evaluate possible benefits of computerized decision support early in a project and set goals to achieve some of them. Once a project is complete, it is important to review the intended benefits and measure how well the project is delivering them.

Following are nine potential benefits and advantages of computerized decision support:

1. *Enhance Decision-Making Effectiveness.* A major category of benefits is improved decision-making effectiveness and better decisions. Decision quality and decision-making effectiveness are, however, hard to document and measure. Most research has examined soft measures such as perceived decision quality rather than objective measures like financial results. Advocates of BI software often argue that more and better analyses will improve decision making.

2. *Gain a Competitive Advantage.* Vendors frequently cite achieving competitive advantage as a major reason for implementing BI systems, performance management systems, and Web-based DSS. Although it is possible to gain a competitive advantage from computerized decision support, this is not a very likely outcome. Vendors routinely sell the same product to competitors and even help with the installation. Organizations are most likely to gain this advantage from novel, high-risk, enterprise-wide, inward-facing decision support systems. This potential benefit is examined extensively in the next section.

3. *Improve Communication Among Decision Makers.* DSS can improve communication and collaboration among decision makers. In some circumstances, communications-driven and group DSS have had

this impact. Model-driven DSS provides a means for sharing facts, assumptions, and analyses.

4. *Increase Data Accuracy and Data Sharing.* If developers have high-quality data in source systems and are able to integrate it in a common data source, then managers can access "one version of the truth" about company operations. Data-driven and model-driven DSS can access historical data, and system outputs can encourage fact-based decision making. Improving data accessibility and increasing data sharing are often goals of decision support projects.

5. *Increase Decision-Maker Satisfaction.* DSS may reduce frustrations of decision makers, create perceptions that we are using better information, and create perceptions that the individual is a "better" decision maker. Satisfaction is a complex measure and we often measure satisfaction with the DSS interface rather than satisfaction with using a DSS in decision making. Improving satisfaction is a secondary benefit that may not lead to important organization outcomes.

6. *Increase Organizational Control.* Data-driven DSS often make business transaction data available for performance monitoring and ad hoc querying. Such systems can enhance management understanding of business operations, and managers perceive that this is useful. It is not always correct that firms can realize financial benefit from accessing better data.

7. *Promote Decision-Maker Learning.* Learning can occur as a by-product of the initial and then the ongoing use of a specific DSS. Two types of learning seem to occur: learning of new concepts and the development of a better factual understanding of the business and decision making environment. Some DSS serve as *de facto* training tools for new employees.

8. *Reduce Cycle Time.* DSS and decision automation can speed up decisions. Research finds reduced decision cycle time, increased employee productivity, and more timely information for decision making from using specific systems. Cycle time refers to the elapsed time from when a decision process begins until it is completed.

9. *Reduce Decision Process Costs.* Some research and especially vendor case studies have documented computerized decision support cost

savings associated with reduced labor costs in making decisions and from lower infrastructure or technology costs.

Decision support, analytics, and BI applications can help managers proactively make informed, actionable decisions and improve performance across the enterprise. Decision support applications can increase agility, helping managers move quickly and easily to respond to customers and change. Software vendors make these claims and they are the "best case" scenario when design and implementation of decision support capabilities meet expectations.

Managers need to be proactive and anticipate consequences. Performance monitoring and model-driven DSS can assist in that task. Analytics can help managers and staff act quickly with an actionable decision. Communications-driven DSS can speed up and encourage collaboration. If managers use well-designed DSS, performance should improve. Agility can come from short cycle times, as well as faster access to information. So the potential benefits of decision support are many, but managers must have realistic, understandable expectations.

Can Decision Support Provide a Competitive Advantage?

One of the most common vendor claims for decision support, analytics, and BI systems is that an organization will gain a competitive advantage. Rarely is this claim moderated with words such as "may," "can," or even "should," rather than "will." Such technology optimism creates unrealistic expectations and in some cases contributes to technology cynicism.

Some consultants do temper or moderate the claimed benefits. For example, "A data warehouse can be a competitive advantage dream or a costly nightmare." A more sophisticated marketing message explains one way a firm can gain a competitive advantage: "Data warehousing can provide a competitive advantage for organizations by increasing market share through analysis of customer profiles." Explaining how the advantage will be gained is important if managers are to evaluate the claim.

A recent study by Professor Tom Davenport, director of research for Babson Executive Education at Babson College, suggests that competitive advantage is possible from decision support. Davenport states, "The ability to make business decisions based on tightly focused, fact-based analysis is emerging as a measurable competitive edge in the global economy." Further, Davenport says, "Organizations that fail to invest in the proper analytic technologies will be unable to compete in a fact-based business environment."[1] Davenport draws his conclusions from interviews with 40 C-level executives and directors at 25 globally competitive organizations. Decision support and analytic technologies can provide organizations a competitive edge.

A layperson's definition of an "advantage" involves having a better financial position, better resources, more skills, or a benefit that has resulted from a prior course of action. When exploited competitively, an advantage should help achieve favorable results. A sustainable competitive advantage means an organization does something important much better than competitors and managers expect it to continue. For example, firms can gain an advantage from having superior information technology and better information resources. Some question if such an advantage is sustainable. Most strategy researchers agree that effective use of information can provide a sustainable competitive advantage. In some situations, making better, faster, and more effective decisions can actually create "decision superiority."[2]

If a proposed DSS meets three criteria, then it can potentially create a competitive advantage for an organization. First, managers must be willing to use it and the system must become a significant strength and capability of the organization. Second, the DSS must be unique and proprietary to the organization. Third, it seems likely the advantage provided by the DSS must be sustainable until the organization receives an adequate payback on its investment. Managers who are searching for strategic investments in information technology need to keep these three criteria in mind. Just because a vendor says a product will create a competitive advantage does not make the claim true.

The widespread use of computer technology has changed the way companies do business. Information technology has altered relationships between companies and their suppliers, customers, and rivals. Porter and Millar discuss two specific ways that information technology can affect competition: by altering industry structures and by supporting cost or differentiation strategies, or both.[3] A common approach used to identify opportunities to change the structure and profitability of an industry is to examine five competitive forces. Michael Porter argued that the power of buyers, the power of suppliers, the threat of new entrants, the threat of substitute products, and the rivalry among existing competitors determines the profitability of an industry. How a company uses information technology can affect each of the five competitive forces and can create the need and opportunity for change.[4]

Information technology has altered the bargaining relationships between companies and their suppliers, channels, and buyers. Today, information systems can easily cross company boundaries. These interorganizational systems have become common and, in some instances, changed the boundaries of the participating industries. DSS can reduce the power of buyers and suppliers. DSS can erect new barriers that reduce the threat of entrants. Implementing a DSS can help differentiate products and services and reduce the threat from substitutes. In addition, DSS can help managers assess the cost of rivalry actions.

Decision support can potentially help a firm create a cost advantage. DSS can provide many benefits including improving personal efficiency and reducing staff needs, expediting problem solving, and increasing organizational control. Managers who want to create a cost advantage should search for situations where decision processes seem slow or tedious and where problems reoccur or solutions are delayed or unsatisfactory. In some cases, DSS can reduce costs where decision makers have high turnover and training is slow and cumbersome, and in situations where activities, departments, and projects are poorly controlled.

DSS can create a major cost advantage by increasing decision-making efficiency or eliminating value chain activities. For example, a bank or mortgage loan firm may reduce costs by using a new DSS to consolidate the number of steps and minimize the number of staff hours needed to approve loans. Technology breakthroughs can sometimes continue to lower costs, and rivals who imitate an innovative DSS may quickly negate any advantage.

Decision support can potentially create a differentiation advantage. Providing a DSS to customers can differentiate a product and possibly provide a new service. Differentiation of products and services increases profitability when the price premium charged is greater than any added costs associated with achieving the differentiation. Successful differentiation means a firm can charge a premium price, sell more units, or increase buyer loyalty for service, or increase repeat purchases. In some situations, competitors can rapidly imitate the differentiation, and then all competitors incur increased costs for implementing the capability.

Finally, decision support can be used to help an organization better focus on a specific customer segment and hence gain an advantage in meeting that segment's needs. Management information systems and decision support systems can help track customers, and DSS can make it easier to serve a specialized customer group with special services. Some customers will not pay a premium for targeted service, and large competitors target specialized niches using their own DSS.

Some firms have no competitive advantage. Firms can achieve a competitive advantage by making strategic changes, and firms can lose a competitive advantage when competitors make strategic changes. Implementing computerized decision support does not necessarily create a competitive advantage. In fact, most decision support does not have such a broad enterprise-wide impact.

Decision support can be strategically important, useful and very necessary, and yet not provide a competitive advantage. Many consulting firms and vendors focus on gaining competitive advantage from a DW or a BI system, and that can happen. Many BI projects do not deliver such results.

A now classic study, Kettinger et al., identified a number of companies that had gained an advantage from information systems.[5] Some systems were decision support systems. For example, Air Products created a vehicle scheduling system, Cigna implemented a risk assessment system, IBM built a marketing management system, Owens–Corning deployed a materials selection system, and Procter & Gamble used a customer response system. It is very likely that competitor responses and technology changes have had a negative impact on these systems. Publicizing that a DSS has provided an advantage encourages competitors to duplicate the system.

If a company is trying to develop a decision support or BI system that provides a competitive advantage, managers and analysts should ask how the proposed system affects company costs, customer and supplier relations, and managerial effectiveness. Managers should also attempt to assess how the proposed system may change the structure of the industry and the behavior of competitors. Finally, managers must continuously invest in and improve information and decision support technologies to maintain any competitive advantage.

Can DSS Impact Decision Outcomes?

Building a computerized DSS does not necessarily improve decision outcomes. The end result of actions is a function of the actions, not the tools used to evaluate possible actions. Sadly, a poorly constructed DSS or analytic application can actually reduce decision quality and lead to suboptimal actions. DSS impact decision outcomes only when better actions are selected, but a system may have secondary benefits, such as faster decision making or reduced training costs for new decision makers. Some DSS actually increase the likelihood that targeted users will make "good" decisions. At issue in answering this question is defining decision success and understanding how decision support can improve decision processes or the information content in a situation and hence help users make more "good" decisions and have better outcomes.

Good decisions are the ones that resolve an identified problem or that result in the best possible outcome in a situation. Many decisions do not have this intended outcome. No manager always makes the right decision. Factors that are unforeseeable or over which the decision maker has little or no control assure some wrong decisions, for example, bad weather, disease, changing economic conditions, false information received, bad luck, and changes in laws and regulations. We hope a well-constructed DSS positively improves decision outcomes and increases the likelihood of "good" decisions.

According to Trull, the success of a decision is a function of its quality and of how well it is implemented.[6] We can judge decision quality by examining a decision's compatibility with existing constraints, its timeliness, and its incorporation of the optimal amount of information. A successful implementation results when managers (a) avoid conflict of interest, (b) make sure everyone involved understands the decision, and

(c) explain how rewards of a successful implementation are worth the risks. Improved decisions result from more effective decision processes. DSS can improve the quality of information used by a decision maker and improve the decision process to positively impact decision outcomes.

Some decision aids, BI systems, and DSS have failed to improve decision making. Computer applications can provide a false sense of confidence that information is complete or that data is accurate. Completeness and accuracy of decision-relevant information are important concerns. Developers need to design and implement appropriate DSS, analytics, and BI to positively change decision outcomes.

What Are Substitutes for Computerized Decision Support?

In many situations, computerized decision support is a necessity, but there remain many substitutes, complements, and alternative approaches for improving decision making. In addition, situational factors can reduce or mitigate the need for computerized decision support. In the late 1970s, Kerr and Jermier suggested that substitutes existed for leadership.[7] In 1978, it was "fiction" to think that computerized decision support could substitute for leadership, but vendors have made progress in using computers to assist leaders. It is important to remember that outstanding leaders and decision makers can reduce the need to deploy computerized decision support. Leaders made effective decisions for thousands of years without the assistance of computers.

A substitute is a replacement. The substitute action or approach takes the place of a computerized solution and serves the same function. Some substitutes work almost as well as a computerized solution, others are poor replacements. A complement increases the effectiveness of the decision support capability.

Today the increasing complexity and uncertainty in many organizational decision situations, coupled with time pressures and heavy information loads, provide a justification for the development of operational, tactical, and strategic DSS. Computerized decision support is not, however, always the best or the only solution for improving and enhancing decision making in admittedly difficult circumstances. There are a number of potential substitutes and complements to using computerized decision support. Some substitute factors make computerized DSS less necessary, but result in high costs and create other problems, while other factors are often "enhancers" or complements when used in conjunction with DSS to improve decision making.

Kerr suggested that certain situational factors or variables reduce the importance of formal leadership and even substitute for leadership. Such a substitution phenomenon also seems to occur in many decision situations and various factors alter the need for computerized decision support. Kerr, Jermier, and others focused on subordinate, task, and organizational characteristics as potential substitutes for effective leader behavior and actions. In a similar way, task, organizational, and environment characteristics change the need for computerized decision support. Characteristics of managers and their subordinates also impact the need for and use of computerized DSS.

So what factors can substitute for computerized decision support? Let us examine twelve factors that can be altered to impact the need for computerized decision support. Specific factors help decision makers cope with important, complex, decision-making tasks. As a caveat, the following list may be incomplete and overlapping. It is not an ordered or prioritized list, rather it is more of an alphabetized list based on research and brainstorming.

1. *Altering Decision Authority and Centralization.* In a specific situation, altering the authority of decision makers changes the need for and usefulness of a DSS. The power of third parties, organization policies, and legal, political, and social constraints limit decision authority and change decision support requirements. If a crisis occurs, decisions may be made at only the highest levels in an organization. In this situation, the requirements change. In more routine situations, a DSS encourages delegation of decisions. To avoid using computer support for time critical decisions, it is sometimes possible to delegate such decisions to a person with "real-time" knowledge. This happens with first responders and customer support staff.

2. *Changing Decision Speed Expectations.* In some situations, increasing or extending the decision cycle—the time spent making a

decision—can reduce the need for computerized decision support. Increasing the cycle time may help decision makers to make "fewer," better decisions without harming the overall outcomes. For example, if a company has competitive and market superiority, it may be possible to slow down new product introductions or reduce advertising expenditures and improve the success of such activities. Reducing time pressure and more analysis can sometimes increase decision effectiveness and reduce the need for computerized support.

3. *Changing Decision Task Structure.* Some decision tasks are needlessly complex. If a person or group with less knowledge and skill completes the task, we need decision support to maintain or improve task proficiency. For example, the task of configuring computer systems at Digital Equipment (DEC) became very complex, and a knowledge-driven DSS called XCON, expert configuror, was built to help with the task. An alternative used by competitors was to simplify the configuration and decision task. Characteristics of a decision task change the need for decision support. For example, managers completing an unambiguous, routine, and highly structured decision task may have only a limited need for computerized decision support. In addition, if decision makers receive fast, frequent feedback concerning the success of their decisions, then they may improve decision quality without any decision support.

4. *Formalization of Procedures.* Business rules, planning processes, procedures, and policies support decision making. Characteristics of the organization setting, especially formalization of rules and processes, alter the need for DSS. For example, in addition to rules and procedures, written plans and goals can reduce the need for computerized decision support. If the rule is, "The customer is always right and we accept all returns," then we do not need computerized decision support to help customer service representatives. Once a crisis or event triggers a need for a decision, contingency plans can reduce the need for computerized decision support. Any negative anchoring effect of having contingency plans is often more than outweighed by the "speed" and quality of preparation advantages than are achieved. We can improve contingency planning using appropriate DSS. For

example, a knowledge-driven DSS with a document repository can support contingency planning.

5. *Increasing Work Load and Effort.* Long hours by staff and decision makers can substitute for a DSS or compensate for a "poor" DSS, but fatigue can lead to major errors and staff burnout. Even with DSS, decision making in a crisis is hard, "mentally taxing," stressful work. The goal in complex, strategic or crisis decision situations, or both, is to have decision support technology help increase the likelihood of success and hopefully reduce stress.

6. *Leaders and Staffing.* Changing leaders and managers may reduce the need for decision support. It may be possible to identify people who make better decisions in the decision environment. Some people are better able to remain calm and focused in complex situations and hence will need less computerized decision support or be better able to use what decision support is provided. Leadership is about having the respect and trust of those who will act based on directions. Decision support cannot substitute for poor managers or weak leaders, but outstanding leaders may require less elaborate or even different decision support. Leadership skills can substitute for some computerized decision support capabilities. Characteristics of managers and their subordinates that impact the need for and usefulness of computerized decision support include ability, experience, training, and knowledge.

7. *Operations Technology.* Production systems can add complexity to decision tasks. Altering the production and operation technology can simplify decision tasks and reduce the need for decision support. For example, implementing a flexible manufacturing system may reduce the need for large batch manufacturing operations and hence model-driven forecasts.

8. *Slack Resource Creation.* Slack is a measure of excess capacity or supply. For example, to reduce the need for inventory management and supply chain decision support, one can keep large safety stocks and centralize inventory. The trade-off is of course higher inventory holding costs.

9. *Staffing Level Increases.* In some situations, as decision complexity and decision volume increase, it is possible to increase the number

of expert decision makers (e.g., add more truck dispatchers or air traffic controllers). More staff can reduce the need for computerized decision support for complex operations by increasing the amount of human decision support. Conversely, computerized decision support can eliminate decision roles in processes and streamline the process, thereby freeing up experts for other tasks.

10. *Training Decision Makers.* Managers who are well-prepared to perform a specific decision task and who have rehearsed the decision making, are more likely to be successful. Training can complement or substitute for decision support.

11. *Use General Purpose Computer Software Tools.* To substitute for using task-specific decision support, but gain some benefits of computerization, one can often use commercial off-the-shelf personal productivity software like Microsoft Excel, Word, or PowerPoint. Personal productivity software is very useful and it provides some generalized decision support.

12. *Use Non-Computerized Decision Aids.* Managers have used and continue to use a wide range of non-computerized decision support tools including maps, calculators, and check lists to assist in decision making. Decision support can be provided without using a computer.

The above approaches and situational changes can sometimes substitute for computerized decision support. Most often, we use a combination of the above factors with decision support and information technologies to support and improve decision making.

Managers need to understand the strengths and limitations of computerized decision support. Formalization may be a good substitute for a data-driven DSS for performance monitoring or a complement that increases usage. A checklist may substitute for a knowledge-driven DSS. More face-to-face meetings and travel may substitute for a communications-driven DSS. Paper-based filing cabinets substitute for document-driven DSS. Calculating a solution or bid amount manually may substitute for a model-driven, cost estimation DSS developed using Excel.

Key lessons from examining substitutes are: (a) decision makers must maintain an ability to function effectively in decision-making situations with or without computerized decision support, and (b) managers must make trade-offs in using technology to support decision-making tasks.

What Are the Possible Disadvantages of Building and Using DSS?

DSS can create advantages for organizations and have positive benefits, but building and using DSS can create negative outcomes in some situations. Managers often need to trade off advantages and disadvantages of a proposed system. For example, some data-driven DSS development efforts lead to power struggles over who should have access to data. In another situation, managers may have personal motives for advocating development of a specific DSS that harms other managers or the organization as a whole. My discussion of disadvantages builds upon the work of Klein and Methie, and Winograd and Flores.[8] Table 6.1 summarizes advantages and disadvantages of DSS. The following discusses the eight disadvantages:

1. *Assumption of Relevance.* According to Winograd and Flores, managers assume that the topics a computerized DSS can deal with are the most relevant issues. This assumption is sometimes false. So there is a danger that managers will use decision support inappropriately. Training for managers about the purpose and use of a system is the only way to avoid this potential problem.

Table 6.1. Advantages and Disadvantages of Implementing DSS

Advantages	Disadvantages
Enhance decision-making effectiveness	Assumption of relevance
Gain a competitive advantage	False belief in objectivity
Improve communication among decision makers	Information overload
Increase data accuracy and data sharing	Obscuring responsibility
Increase decision-maker satisfaction	Overemphasize decision making
Increase organizational control	Status reduction
Promote decision-maker learning	Transfer of power
Reduce cycle time	Unanticipated effects
Reduce decision process costs	

2. *False Belief in Objectivity.* Managers who use computerized decision support may not be more objective and rational in their decision making. Computer software can encourage more rational actions, but managers can also use decision support technologies to rationalize their actions.

3. *Information Overload.* A poorly designed DSS increases information load. Although excessive information load can be a problem, DSS can help managers organize and use information. Computerized decision support can actually reduce and manage information load. Developers need to try to measure the information load created by a system. DSS users need to monitor their perceptions of how much information they are receiving. Handheld, wireless computing devices and smartphones may exacerbate this problem and disadvantage.

4. *Obscuring Responsibility.* Computer software does not make a bad decision; people built the system and chose to use it. Unfortunately some people deflect personal responsibility and blame computerized decision support for mistakes. Computerized decision support is an intermediary between the people who built the system and the people who use the system. The responsibility associated with making a decision using computer support resides with the people who built the system and those who use it.

5. *Overemphasize Decision Making.* Implementing computerized decision support reinforces the rational decision-making perspective and it emphasizes the importance of decision processes and decision making. In many situations, managers need to examine the broader context of decision making and the social, political, and emotional factors that impact organizational success. Managers must examine when and under what circumstances decision support should be built and used. We must continue to ask if a decision situation is appropriate for using any type of decision support.

6. *Status Reduction.* Some managers are concerned that using computerized decision support diminishes their status and forces them to do mundane clerical work. Managers and IS staff who advocate building and using computerized decision support need to deal with any status issues that may arise.

7. *Transfer of Power.* Building computerized decision support, especially knowledge-driven DSS and decision automation, may be perceived as transferring decision authority from managers to a software program. This is more a concern with decision automation systems than with DSS, analytics, and BI.[9] Most managers believe there is an ongoing need for human discretion and innovation in many decision-making processes.

8. *Unanticipated Effects.* Implementing decision support technologies may have unanticipated consequences. Some decision support reduces the skill levels needed to perform a decision task. Some DSS overload decision makers with information and actually reduce decision-making effectiveness. Nevertheless, most negative consequences of decision support seem correctable, avoidable, or subject to remedy.

Conclusions and Summary

There are many decision support advantages and disadvantages so managers must consider trade-offs. DSS can enhance decision-making effectiveness, improve communication among decision makers, reduce decision process costs, increase decision-maker satisfaction, and promote decision-maker learning. DSS, analytics, and BI can improve decision outcomes. However, building a computerized decision support system does not always improve decision outcomes.

Improved decisions result from more effective decision processes. In some situations, it is more appropriate to implement substitutes for computerized decision support, rather than new or more computerized support. We may want to decentralize decision making, or change decision cycle time expectations, or alter the decision task structure instead of building a DSS. The characteristics of a decision task do change the need for decision support. In some situations the best way to improve decision making is to improve training. An analysis of a decision support project proposal is incomplete unless you consider the disadvantages of implementing computerized decision support.

CHAPTER 7

Identifying Decision Support Opportunities

Once a manager concludes it is possible to gain significant benefits, or even a competitive advantage, from building an innovative decision support capability, then it is important to initiate a systematic search process. A search can identify opportunities, significant decision process problems, and decision maker needs. As part of a search, systematic decision process audits, working with consultants, and brainstorming sessions can identify opportunities. In addition to search and investigation, some creativity and forward thinking are important in identifying opportunities.

Many organizations have obsolete, legacy decision support capabilities. A 1990s state-of-the-art capability should be upgraded or more likely replaced. In many organizations, managers and IT staff need to start planning for next generation systems and aggressively search for innovative opportunities. This chapter discusses a search and planning process, clarifies auditing decision processes, examines the content of a feasibility study, and discusses both reengineering concerns and outsourcing.

What Is Decision Support Planning?

There are many IS or IT (IS/IT) planning processes and analysis frameworks such as the traditional strengths, weaknesses, opportunities, and threats (SWOT) analysis—or gap analysis—that might help find decision support opportunities. An information systems planning process should provide a systematic method of searching for and evaluating IS/IT opportunities including decision support. The IS/IT planning must be linked to business-level strategic planning, and the process should be ongoing and open-ended. Planning should identify goals and objectives for decision support. Managers need to collect competitive intelligence, fund DSS research and development projects, conduct regular brainstorming sessions, and in some cases follow hunches and intuition about using technology to improve or accelerate decision making. Companies should have a written decision support plan.

A good technology planning process should examine the technology infrastructure to determine what is currently possible, and examine enhancements that would facilitate or enable new decision support capabilities. Decision support planning should involve broad consultation and both problem-oriented and opportunistic search. DSS do not always solve specific problems; rather, DSS may create new capabilities for customers, suppliers, or even members of the board of directors of a company. A good description of the new capability and a scenario explaining the use of the DSS can help in understanding the benefits. In some situations, an opportunity analysis recommends a "buy" decision because industry-specific decision support packages are available. This type of off-the-shelf DSS may be appropriate, but the resulting DSS will not be innovative and it probably will not provide a competitive advantage.

One approach for finding innovative decision support opportunities is to monitor technology trends and identify DSS innovations in other industries or in consumer markets. Another approach is to identify the tactical and strategic decisions that make a major difference in the success of the business. Then managers should conduct a decision process review and monitor the effectiveness of those decisions. Sometimes a close examination of how a decision is made creates insight and an "ah ha" experience that leads to decision support innovation.

In addition, asking employees for suggestions about ways to improve decision making may highlight opportunities. Employees who observe the results of decisions, suffer from poor processes, or hear the "wrath of customers" may have insights that lead to decision support innovation.

Finally, talk to vendor salespeople. This is useful, but managers need to keep in mind that their inquiry is initiating a selling process. The vendor representative shares what he or she knows about best practices to help identify the manager's needs for decision support. The salesperson will be trying to identify a major need and gap in current decision support.

Once you identify the gap between existing and desired decision support, a good salesperson will try to identify solutions that his or her company has that can fill all or part of the gap. At some point, a vendor representative will explain how the manager can solve the decision support gap. Remember, the vendor salesperson's goal is selling software and services and having a satisfied customer. The best customer for computerized decision support is a knowledgeable manager who asks good questions.

Decision support technology is changing and evolving very rapidly. MIS managers, business managers, and academics face a difficult challenge trying to stay abreast of those changes in order to make good, informed decisions about building and maintaining decision support systems for organizations.

Managers must determine who a proposed decision support capability will support and whether they will use a proposed DSS. Equally important, the champion of the project must know the desired result from using an innovative system. The bottom line is that an innovative DSS must create value. Decision support planning usually becomes more sophisticated as managers experience success with using IT to support decision making.

What Is a Decision Process Audit?

Increasing decision-making effectiveness should be the major objective for any decision support project. Stabell argues "analysis and diagnosis prior to design are key activities in a decision-oriented approach" for building DSS.[1] A decision process audit is one way to diagnose current decision-making problems and specify changes in decision processes. An audit can provide important information for designing a computerized DSS.

In general, auditing operational and managerial decision processes can be very useful. Describing and explaining a specific decision process can be difficult, however, because of problems in defining the boundary of the process. A decision process refers to the steps, tasks, methods, procedures, events and analyses, that lead to a result, a decision. Many decision processes are part of larger processes.

An example of a decision process is described by Hammer and Champy.[2] They describe a process at IBM Credit that is a classic example of a poorly designed decision process. After receiving a call from a salesperson requesting financing, the request is logged on a paper form. After moving that paper around in four more steps, a decision to approve or not is finally made. The entire process "consumed six days on average, although it sometimes took as long as two weeks." The example also illustrates that reengineering can improve decision processes. The structure of the process was changed, improved decision support was developed, and the turnaround on a request for financing was reduced to four hours. Productivity improved dramatically.

An audit is a first step in identifying opportunities to redesign decision processes and include new decision aids, analytics, and DSS in business processes. In some situations, an audit suggests changes in decision technologies that can improve performance and reduce costs. When we complete an audit the two central questions are: (a) how can we do better, and (b) what changes in decision processes, if any, should have the highest priority?

Five steps should occur in a company-wide decision process audit:

Step 1. Defining the decisions, decision processes, and related business processes that will be audited. Define the authority of the auditor, purpose of the audit, scope of the audit, timing of the audit, and resources required to perform the audit. Identify the owner and primary contact for each major decision process.

Step 2. Examining the formal design of each major process. Make diagrams of each process and specify the decision criteria currently used.

Step 3. Examining the actual behavior during the decision process. Observe how the process works. Interview decision makers and collect data. Is the process used as it was intended?

Step 4. Assessing performance of actual decision processes. What works? Can cycle time be reduced? Are decisions appropriate? Timely? Cost effective? Is the process producing value and achieving business objectives? If not, why? The goal is to determine if a decision process is effective and efficient.

Step 5. Preparing a report and recommendations. Summarize steps 1–4 in a written report. Discuss what is working well and what needs to be improved. Develop recommendations for improving major decision processes. Share findings with decision makers.

Both, managers and MIS staff need to work on completing this diagnostic task. In most situations, an audit provides sufficient information to specify a decision support solution.

Is Reengineering Necessary to Build an Effective DSS?

Some business decision processes have serious problems that can be resolved by implementing computerized decision support. In other situations, the decision process has flaws that must be corrected, and some processes must be completely reengineered. However, reengineering is not required to build an effective DSS. Identification and recognition of a lack of computerized decision support in a process does not mean that any decision-making problems would be fixed by implementing decision support. Decision support does not solve all problems.

Hammer and Champy defined business process reengineering as the fundamental rethinking of business processes to achieve dramatic improvements in critical, contemporary measures of performance such as cost, quality, and cycle time.[3] In a now classic *Harvard Business Review* article, Hammer asserted that companies rarely achieve radical performance improvements when they invest in IT. Most companies use computers to speed up, not break away from, business processes and rules that are out of date. Hammer said the power of computers can only be released by reengineering work.[4]

A business process is a group of activities that create value for a customer. Let us briefly examine the process of fulfilling a customer order. Order fulfillment is a process that consists of many activities, starting with order entry, picking products from inventory, dealing with back orders, shipping products, and dealing with returns. A number of decisions are made during the process, but they are primarily routine and recurring. Some metadecisions about product quality or employee performance are made periodically. If we reengineer this overall process, our goal is dramatic improvement in the satisfaction of the customer. We could in turn focus only on the decision to accept or reject a product return and refund or credit the customer's account. Focusing on this important decision may not create a dramatic improvement in customer satisfaction, but it may be a significant improvement. The cost and risk of reengineering may encourage managers to emphasize incremental redesign.

Reengineering does not guarantee effective decision processes. In general, unless there is an influential champion for reengineering a broad business process, it seems most appropriate to focus narrowly on an important decision process embedded in a broader business process. The following tips for redesigning specific decision processes and developing a new computerized DSS should help ensure that decision makers benefit from IT intervention.

1. *Focus on Outcomes for a Narrow Decision Process.* Determine if any type DSS can help improve decision making or reduce cycle time. In particular, determine if computerized support can help gather, organize, or retrieve information systematically, present possible consequences of actions, or support collaboration. Decision makers must understand how capabilities in a proposed DSS will support decision making.

2. *Evaluate Time Pressures.* The greater the time pressure is to make a decision, the worse a person's decision is likely to be. Therefore, computerized decision support should help a user rapidly obtain enough information to make a high quality decision. In particular, any tactical DSS should help a user analyze information, help get other people involved when necessary, and help a user explore available options. A decision process analysis should look for such opportunities.

3. *Check for Ambiguity.* A computerized DSS should help a manager cope with ambiguity. Some decision makers suffer from "analysis paralysis." DSS help conduct appropriate analyses, not promote excessive analysis.

4. *Evaluate Confidence of Decision Makers.* Confident decision makers are more likely to successfully deal with opportunities and risks. Managers need to use their decision-making skills to make the best decision and then use persuasion skills to sell the decision.

Decision processes do become outdated and need periodic review. Adding IT to a poor decision process is generally a mistake. Choosing radical process change is also often a mistake. In many situations the solution involves incremental redesign, improving an existing decision support capability, or introducing limited decision automation. Incrementally improving decision processes can significantly improve decision quality and reduce decision cycle time.

To develop effective computerized decision support of any type, managers and analysts must focus on the interface between the decision maker and the computer. An interface must be responsive to user needs rather than designed solely for efficiency. The most helpful information may result from exploring and sensitivity analysis rather than quick, efficient analysis or data retrieval.

Managers should not focus solely on reengineering decision processes; what we often need is a redesigned decision process with improved IT decision support.

What Is a Decision Support Feasibility Study?

Managers may have ideas for upgrading a DSS or for an innovative decision support capability. Perhaps a senior manager says "it would be great if we could do X?" or "I want X, figure out how to do it"; perhaps someone in the IT group attends a workshop or conference and hears of a system from a colleague or a vendor representative. People nurture some of these ideas, and others are quickly rejected. At some point, a decision support idea becomes concrete enough and the anticipated costs and risks seem tractable so that a potential project champion says, "let's conduct a feasibility study."

An idea for a decision support capability is an abstraction that must become concrete before it is possible to conduct a systematic analysis. Sometimes a feasibility analysis focuses on "go or no go," at other times an analysis compares concept A to concept B, and sometimes the comparison is to "no change" in current practices.

A feasibility study is an analysis that evaluates and documents a contemplated project's viability. Feasibility study also refers to the resulting written document. A feasibility study should help a potential project sponsor make a funding decision or obtain funding.

Following diagnosis of a decision-making process, preliminary design activities often lead to preparation of a feasibility study of the technical and economic prospects for a proposed DSS. This study should occur before actually committing significant resources to developing a proposed system.

An extensive feasibility study for a broad scope decision support project examines many issues, such as proposed scope, targeted users and their needs, anticipated DSS impacts, benefits, and risks. Shorter, less comprehensive studies and reports are usually prepared for small scope decision support projects. Scope refers to the purpose, amount of expenditure, and number of potential users.

A feasibility analysis is a systematic way of exploring the factors and risks affecting the potential for successful development and implementation of a DSS. Large-scale information systems development efforts typically include a feasibility study as a major checkpoint about whether it is possible to develop a system, given the project's goals and constraints. The actual report should provide information about the range of issues likely to affect success and, therefore, that should be considered in decisions about *whether* and *how* to move forward with a decision support development effort.

A Decision Support Feasibility Study should examine site readiness, technical feasibility, and overall financial feasibility. Site readiness determines whether the organization is ready for, and is interested in, implementing a new or revitalized DSS.

Technical feasibility examines in a broad sense whether the project is possible. In some computerized decision support proposals, technical issues are the major risk concern. The stability and maturity of the proposed technology should be reviewed. Using emerging technologies for large scope, poorly structured projects increases risks, but such projects may have large strategic payoffs. Technology optimism is always a danger, and IT managers should evaluate emerging technologies carefully.

Financial feasibility estimates the projected costs of implementing the proposed DSS, and asks whether potential benefits justify these costs. It is important to examine the economic impact of a proposed system. Project leaders and sponsors should identify both tangible and intangible costs and benefits.[5]

Managers should conduct the feasibility analysis in the context of relevant organization goals, constraints, related projects, business decision support needs, priorities, and a decision support diagnosis.

For each proposed decision support solution, some concrete details will need to be specified, including broad system design, system integration issues, major functions and capabilities provided, technology tools/ infrastructure used, and any new organizational structures and processes required.

Some sources also suggest examining schedule feasibility, cultural feasibility, legal feasibility, and operational feasibility. The larger the scope of the proposed project, the more comprehensive the analysis that is required.

A feasibility study should ask key questions and document the answers. Does the project fit with the current IS/IT plan? Do we have the internal skills to manage the project or actually build it? How much time is available to build the new system? Will building the DSS interfere with current business operations? What resources are required and when? What are the overall costs and benefits of each alternative? Can we manage the risk associated with the proposed project? Do we have a conceptual design we can share with funding sources? If the answer is negative or uncertain for too many feasibility questions, then the proposed DSS project should be abandoned or postponed.

Decision support design usually involves a number of difficult trade-offs. The first trade-off is whether a DSS should support both the existing process and a prescribed new process. There is also a trade-off about the extent of the capabilities of the DSS and the scope of the process supported. In most cases the initial version of a DSS focuses on either extensive capabilities for a narrow scope process or few capabilities for a broad scope process.

In all evaluations, one needs to consider the longer-term consequences and not solely immediate cost savings and decision process-time improvements. DSS may reduce some costs, but that is not usually the motivating factor for a new system. A decision support project decision should not be made in isolation from the overall IT project portfolio.

What Factors Influence DSS Implementation Risk?

Managers should identify and evaluate a wide range of decision support projects. Perhaps an enterprise-wide, data warehouse-based DSS should be built to improve reporting and analysis, or a knowledge-driven DSS project to increase staffing fairness and consistency, or a Web-based, model-driven decision support tool to reduce stockouts and minimize obsolete inventory. Decision support projects have varying risk levels and differing risk/reward trade-offs. Managers must assess project risk issues.

Two broad, aggregated factors that impact implementation failure risk are (a) project *scope,* and (b) project *structure. Scope* refers to the breadth of purpose of the DSS, anticipated project budget size, the anticipated number of end users, and the anticipated number of organization units with users of the system. For example, an enterprise-wide, performance monitoring DSS project has broader scope than a department data mart. *Structure* refers to decision task clarity and specificity. High structure means project goals are clearly stated and understandable. A realistic project schedule and a project manager's experience should increase perceptions of project structure.

In general, user expectations, project budget, DSS architecture, project requirements, IT priorities, technology understanding, and data needs influence an assessment of project scope. Management commitment, schedules, staff training, project manager skills, organization structures, and procedures influence an assessment of project structure.

Decision support projects have various levels of risk associated with them. When DSS projects have ambiguous goals and low structure, the projects have higher levels of risk of failure because the project's costs and scope of work are harder to define. In addition, because the objectives and purpose of the project are ambiguous, it can be difficult to assess the return on the investment. DSS projects with a higher degree of structure and more clearly defined objectives generally are lower risk and more likely to be successfully completed. More detailed planning is possible for projects with specific objectives, and good plans lower risk. Finally, the sophistication of the technology and the experience of the developers using the technology influence the overall project failure risk.

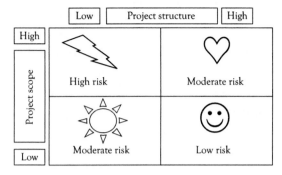

Figure 7.1. Project implementation risk matrix.

Innovative decision support involves lower structure and inherently has moderate-to-high failure risk.

If we consider project scope and structure in a 2×2 matrix, then low scope and high structure projects have low risk. High scope and low structure projects have high levels of risk. The other two situations generally have moderate levels of implementation risk.

Some studies estimate that over one-half of all IT projects are over budget, late, or do not deliver the expected scope.[6] We want to reduce this risk. Good project management reduces or mitigates some risk factors during implementation. We can assess some risk factors before the start of a project, and hence potentially manage them. During project implementation, a good project manager continually monitors risk factors. The following are some questions for managers to ask before approving a decision support project:

1. How much project and project portfolio risk can the organization accept, tolerate, and manage?
2. Have targeted users helped define project requirements and scope?
3. Does the project have a strong, committed, internal sponsor?
4. Do internal staff understand the proposed technology?
5. Does the budget include contingencies for unanticipated costs, especially infrastructure and process change costs?
6. Is the project plan and schedule understandable and reasonable?
7. Is the project manager experienced with similar scope projects?
8. Has a feasibility study been completed for the project?

Minimizing implementation risk is critical for effective project implementation. The ultimate decision to invest in a decision support project should be based on multiple criteria, not solely on project risk. Sometimes the decision support project that is most likely to result in a competitive advantage is a high-risk project. If appropriately managed, high-risk analytics, BI, or DSS projects can be successfully implemented on time, under budget, and with the originally intended scope and functionality.

What Are the Trade-Offs of Outsourcing Enterprise-Wide DSS?

Some companies outsource major IT activities such as Internet and Intranet operations, data storage and backup, and enterprise applications such as accounting or enterprise resource planning. Outsourcing decision support may involve contracting with consultants, software houses, or service bureaus to perform analysis and design, programming, or other development, delivery and systems management activities. Outsourcing enterprise-wide DSS definitely has risks. Managers need to determine if traditional benefits from IT outsourcing such as more predictable costs, increased innovation, and increased flexibility outweigh the risks of outsourcing an enterprise-wide DSS.

An enterprise-wide DSS is usually a data-driven DSS that supports a large group of managers in a networked client-server environment with a specialized data warehouse as part of the DSS architecture. Outsourcing this type of DSS involves developing a formal agreement with a third party to perform a major part of an organization's decision support function. Outsourcing decision support involves delegating responsibility for building a mission-critical information systems application or its operation, or both, to an outside firm. The outside firm has a financial reason to do a good job, but that may be insufficient. Managers are transferring a vital function previously performed in-house to an outside provider.

For decision support outsourcing to work, it is important to evaluate the outsourcing provider as a long-term asset, and as a source of ongoing value and expertise. To manage the relationship and maximize its value, both significant management time and staff resources need to be dedicated to the relationship. The buyer of outsourced expertise needs a project manager devoted to the outsourcing relationship. The buyer should intend to keep the outsourcing relationship for as long as it provides needed services and creates value. As part of outsourcing, new technology alliances will often need to be formed with vendors. In general, a buyer that outsources decision support should strive to align its provider's motivation with its goals by negotiating appropriate incentives and penalties.

Some of the benefits of outsourcing decision support include potentially lower cost development and deployment, more predictable operations costs, access to expertise about new technologies, and increased flexibility. In addition, outsourcing can free up resources within the firm for other projects.

Outsourcing a DSS project, however, has a number of risks. First, a company relinquishes control of an important capability to an outside organization. Second, contracts for a DSS may be long term and may lock a company into a particular service provider. Finally, reliance on external sources for new systems development can lead to low technical knowledge among the in-house IS/IT staff.

These three major risks often lead to in-house decision support development and operation rather than to outsourcing. When does outsourcing seem to work? Outsourcing can be successful when managers need to improve decision support activities and systems quickly and in-house IS/IT staff seem unable to build innovative DSS.

In general, enterprise-wide DSS targeted at managers should be built in-house and managed as a strategic capability. If a DSS is intended to support key business decisions, then managers should want to reduce any risk that the system will be compromised. It is important that unauthorized individuals are not able to gain access to or tamper with a DSS and its data. In general, in-house development and operation of an enterprise-wide DSS should enhance the security, credibility, and value of the system.

Outsourcing is essentially a make-or-buy decision. Should we perform the service or hire someone else to perform it? Managers need to assess whether any cost savings are worth the risk associated with outsourcing strategic decision support systems. Decision support capabilities are central to the operation and success of many organizations and hence are core competencies[7] that should not be outsourced.

Conclusions and Summary

Decision support planning and a decision process audit can help identify decision support opportunities. It is not necessary to reengineer decision processes to have an effective DSS. In general, managers should consider a wide range of decision support projects. Decision support projects have varying risk levels and differing risk/reward trade-offs. Managers must assess project risk issues that result from differing project scope and project structure. For example, enterprise-wide DSS projects have broader scope than department projects and hence greater risk. The "Project Implementation Risk Matrix" summarizes how risk varies based on project scope and structure. During project implementation, a good project manager continually monitors risk factors. One of the greatest dangers with an innovative decision support project is that the project champion leaves the organization. Outsourcing a strategic DSS can be a major mistake.

CHAPTER 8

Looking Forward to Innovative Decision Support

Technology developments continue to create many opportunities to implement innovative decision support. This is good news for managers who plan to use decision support to help cope with a turbulent environment. The bad news is that many projects will have cost overruns and will not meet expectations. To increase the success rate for decision support, analytics, and business intelligence projects, managers must carefully evaluate proposed projects.

Both managers and MIS professionals are involved in evaluating proposed DSS projects. The technical managers who need to focus on evaluating decision support projects include the chief information officer, corporate IT professionals, database administrators, and network administrators. The business managers evaluating these projects include senior managers, strategic planners, business development managers, competitive intelligence analysts, and market researchers.

When managers evaluate decision support projects, it is important to approach the task with some skepticism and it is necessary to ask the tough questions about costs, benefits, and risks. This chapter examines two types of evaluation activities to be carried out during and after completing a project, potential ethical issues with DSS, the role of a project champion, and next-generation decision support.

When Is Formative Rather than Summative Evaluation Used?

Once a decision support project begins, evaluation activities must continue. A formative evaluation involves judgments and feedback while development activities are occurring. Formative evaluation focuses on how the system design is progressing and measures intermediate outcomes observable during the development process. A summative evaluation involves judgments and feedback at the end of the development process and once the system is in use. The focus of summative evaluation is on assessing whether the system meets expectations and whether it provides desired immediate and longer-term outcomes. In the words of Robert Stakes, "When the cook tastes the soup, that's formative; when the guests taste the soup, that's summative."[1]

Potential decision support users should provide the primary feedback for formative evaluation. The evaluation criteria should emphasize the user interface and usability issues. As part of a formative evaluation of a model-driven DSS, the model needs to be reviewed and validated by an expert. Formative evaluation of a knowledge-driven DSS needs to verify the rules and knowledge base. Examining data and document quality are legitimate issues in the formative evaluation of data or document-driven DSS.

Summative evaluation should include assessments by users and expert evaluators. Evaluation criteria should be broader and managers should assess the impact of the DSS on both decision making and the organization.

Evaluation differs based on when it occurs, the intentions of the evaluator, the intent of the evaluation—formative or summative, and whether an internal or external person does the evaluation.

In both, a formative or a summative evaluation, data from users and potential users should have the major impact on the conclusions. In formative evaluation, the key is to create a positive, constructive feedback loop. If the evaluation suggests that the system cannot be built, then managers need to act quickly to end the project. A positive approach to evaluation can result in ending or improving a decision support project or in discontinuing use or rebuilding a legacy DSS.

What Are Ethical Issues Associated with Building and Using DSS?

Some people think that building or using a computerized decision support capability is ethically neutral. That is certainly not a valid conclusion. Researchers and managers are only beginning to consider and evaluate the ethical choices associated with computerized decision support. Decision support proposals can raise ethical and value issues for builders. Choosing to use or to not use a computerized DSS may itself be an ethical issue. Managers and researchers need to anticipate these ethical issues as we look forward to building and using innovative DSS.

One approach to anticipating ethical issues is to identify plausible critical ethical incidents. So what are some situations that might occur? The following incidents can serve as a starting point for further thought and discussion:

Scenario 1. A builder of a Business Intelligence System chooses not to include a key metric because the data is hard to capture and display. Eventually that metric, for example the weight of a prototype airplane, becomes a critical flaw that leads to major cost overruns.

Scenario 2. A sponsor proposes combining sales and credit card data and a DSS builder becomes concerned that the privacy rights of past customers will be in jeopardy. The sponsor is a powerful figure in the company who does not like dissent.

Scenario 3. A builder realizes that the quality of data for a proposed data-driven DSS is flawed and inaccurate and still proceeds to build the system.

Scenario 4. A builder fails to validate a forecast model used for predictive analytics and people report serious excess inventory problems. The company takes a major write-down on obsolete inventory.

Scenario 5. A user of a data-driven DSS notices a sales problem in a store and drills down into the underlying data. He sees a large transaction by his wife. The user confronts his wife with the information he found using the DSS.

Scenario 6. A manager fails to use a business process monitoring system and a subordinate makes an unauthorized trade. The trade results in significant losses.

Scenario 7. The knowledge base for a knowledge-driven DSS becomes out of date and no one acts to identify or fix the problem. The recommendations become increasingly error-prone and users start ignoring the results from the system.

Scenario 8. During use of a communications-driven DSS, conversations are recorded automatically and users "forget" that is happening. Some negative personal comments are made and a senior manager requests the recording.

Scenario 9. A manager extracts data from a decision support database and transfers the data in an E-mail to a home computer. The home computer is subsequently stolen.

As a senior manager in the firm, what would you do in each situation? Why would you take that action? Many of these ethical scenarios involve difficult choices. Initially the situation may seem clear-cut, but sometimes the constraints encourage choosing an action that is questionable and then other managers choose a remedy that is unethical or vice-versa.

Analysis from a DSS builder perspective. Principles and values play an important role in making many significant organizational decisions. When DSS are constructed, developers make assumptions that can have ethical impacts on user choices. Also, some decisions are considered so value-laden that many people would be uncomfortable with developing a DSS to assist a decision maker. One cannot specify all of the ethical issues that might be relevant to a specific DSS proposal, but once a proposal reaches the feasibility stage, the project sponsor needs to address the ethical issues associated with the project. Also, during development, builders need to be sensitive to how the representations such as charts and tables designed to present information impact the decision maker.

Privacy concerns are also easy to ignore during the evaluation of a DSS proposal. In many societies, people expect that certain personal and behavioral information about them will be kept private. This information belongs to the person and does not belong to a company, the public, or the government. Managers need to ensure that data used in DSS does not infringe on the privacy rights of individuals. The exact extent of privacy rights for employees, customers, and other data providers is not always clearly defined. In general, unless there is a clearly compelling reason to risk violating an individual's privacy, the "fence" to protect privacy of data should exceed any minimum requirements.

Analysis from a managerial perspective. Managers who have access to a DSS as part of their job may have a fiduciary duty to actually use DSS, especially if the system improves decision quality. A fiduciary is expected to provide the "highest standard of care" to the person to whom he/she owes the duty. For example, if an investment advisor or a bank trust officer is not using a DSS, there may be a breach of fiduciary responsibility.

When does using a DSS become a professional requirement of doing a specific job well? Is using a DSS a "prudent practice" in some situations? Are there situations where not using a DSS should be considered malpractice?

Misuse of decision support data is difficult to detect and monitor. For example, a police officer may use a law enforcement database to find out information about a neighbor or friend. Some DSS queries need to be logged so abuse can be monitored. Also, data quality is a problem in some organizations for both users and builders. When is poor data quality so serious that a data-driven DSS should not be built or used? Also, users may make unauthorized file transfers of DSS data that is subsequently misused. How can this be detected or prevented? An ongoing issue for users and builders is what information will be accessible and by whom and when? Written policies must outline access rules and system use permissions and restrictions to reduce ethical lapses and keep poor judgment about data use from leading to additional problems.

The following are some important decision support ethical issues that should be considered:

1. Failing to assure data quality
2. Hidden capture of data
3. Propagating data errors
4. Ongoing use of an obsolete DSS
5. Combining databases and data linking that violates privacy
6. Inappropriate use of customer profiles/data
7. Legal liability issues from failing to use or from misuse of a DSS
8. Excluding data or key metrics because of missing data
9. Failing to validate a quantitative model
10. Unauthorized data transfers
11. Lack of policies or poor policy enforcement.

Company policies should guide the behavior of managers and builders on these topics. Managers should establish policy to help ensure ethical use of DSS. To establish appropriate policies, managers need to discuss the subtleties of a wide variety of ethical situations that builders and users might encounter. When in doubt about the ethical use of a DSS, or the need to use a DSS, or the consequences of poor design decisions on the behavior of the decision makers, do not ignore the issue or concern, rather ask others, consult, and discuss. Ignoring ethical issues associated with building and using computerized decision support is not an option.

Can Project Champions Reduce Resistance to a New System?

A new decision support capability may be an incremental change in an existing process, or provide a radical new way of creating and sharing decision relevant information, or something in between. An innovative DSS is a technology change, and a new DSS will likely encounter resistance to its use from some stakeholders. Managers should anticipate and plan for resistance to using a proposed DSS. Builders and managers championing a project need to act to deal with both rational and emotional concerns of those impacted by the new system. In general, how managers build and deploy a DSS determines the amount of resistance that occurs. Project champions can take actions to reduce resistance to an innovative decision support capability. A number of actions and strategies can reduce resistance to a new DSS.

First, develop and explain a rational justification for the change—share the vision. An analysis of decision support needs involves making assumptions and trade-offs. Rational objections to the change may exist and decision support builders must be open to feedback and dialogue with stakeholders. People often have a healthy skepticism of radical change. If the diagnosis has been systematic and appropriately executed, managers can overcome many objections and concerns of stakeholders.

Second, identify and recruit additional champions for the change. Make sure the advocates understand the pros and cons of the system and are good role models for the new way of making decisions. If the goal is more and better fact-based decision making, make sure a potential champion is known for finding and using facts in current decision situations. Champions can help gain consensus at the beginning of a project and explain the project goals.

Third, demonstrate and communicate project successes. It is important to show short-term progress. Long, delayed decision support implementations create stress and test the commitment of everyone involved.

Fourth, provide training and help people adjust to the new system. The negative consequences of resisting the new system must be much greater than changing to it. Some people may fear they cannot learn the new system, others will fear a loss of status or influence. Change creates new roles and requires new learning. Comfort people and help them adapt.

Various authors[2] identify four broad strategies of change management. The strategies can be used together and include:

1. *Rational Argument Strategy.* Communicate the what, how, and why of a new decision support capability and provide incentives to adopt the system.
2. *Education Strategy.* Use the culture and social norms to reinforce adopting the new system. Provide training and informational materials and develop a commitment to the new decision process.
3. *Coercive Strategy.* Mandate use of a new DSS and impose sanctions on those who do not comply. Change is promoted based on the exercise of authority.
4. *Adaptive/Incremental Strategy.* Alter organizational circumstances, reorganize, and restaff as part of introducing the new DSS. Make small changes and introduce the DSS using pilot or phased deployment.

In general, choose one of the pure strategies or mix of strategies that is matched with situational factors such as: (a) the amount of anticipated resistance, (b) attitudes of the target users, (c) stakes and results associated with success and failure, and (d) urgency of adoption. Using a coercive strategy is often counter-productive.

The existing social system in a company, including how managers make and implement decisions, is usually firmly entrenched. Builders need to begin a new project by understanding and documenting existing decision processes and discussing the effectiveness of the processes with those who currently make the decisions. New DSS cannot be imposed by outside consultants; rather, if possible, the need for a new system must be accepted by all key stakeholders early in the building and design process and then their support must be maintained.

What Is Expected in Next-Generation Decision Support?

Analytics and decision support are important to business success. Developers will create the next generation of computerized decision support with experimentation and technological creativity. Managers and developers will exploit emerging technologies. Innovative technology development is however fraught with problems, but investing in new technology capabilities can be very rewarding. The challenge is to balance the risks and rewards.

All of us should ask what is possible and what is probable in the development of decision support in the near future. Improvements in microprocessor technologies enable the design and development of faster, more graphically sophisticated DSS. Other enabling technologies that have changed and will change possibilities include fast mass storage, display technologies, smartphones, networking, and communication technologies. The leading technology edge seems to foreshadow what will become more widespread decision support capabilities by about five years.

Organizations have developed many computerized systems to support various decision making and planning processes and tasks. Some of the systems have focused on management and operations control, others have focused on financial management, logistics, and planning. DSS assist in complex decision tasks that involve expertise and large amounts of information or that can otherwise benefit from computerized support.

The next step in building more sophisticated decision support exploits some new technologies and emphasizes creating a synergy between users and a DSS that helps a person perform a decision task. What technologies are on the horizon to build more advanced DSS? Grid computing[3] and parallelism in next generation microprocessor chips seem particularly interesting from a decision support perspective; stereographic displays and wearable computing are maturing technologies. Global positioning technology[4] is getting better and radio frequency and wireless devices are becoming more powerful. Stream computing software enables analysis of massive amounts of data in real-time. Open source BI tools[5] and Web 2.0[6] user interface features are changing development environments. Virtual world technologies[7] are improving dramatically. Analysis of big data and especially social network data is much easier. Big data is high volume, high velocity, high variety, and high veracity.[8]

Next generation decision support exploits:

1. a customizable, high resolution, graphics-intensive user interface;
2. dynamic, "real-time," data-driven analysis capabilities;
3. knowledge-driven assistance in real-time;
4. realistic visual simulations that decision makers interact with;
5. small, wearable, wireless computing and communication devices;
6. time, context, and location awareness.

The transformation in decision support associated with Internet and Cloud computing technologies is ongoing. The potential expansion of decision support to mobile devices is only beginning. Managers can expect much better, more targeted, more secure decision support in the years ahead.

Conclusions and Summary

Anticipating the future and the consequences of actions is important in evaluating innovative decision support. Real innovative decision support results from evaluation activities, resolution of potential ethical issues, a visionary project champion, and exploiting next generation capabilities. Potential decision support users should provide the primary feedback for formative evaluation. Managers must conduct summative evaluations of legacy and new systems. Decision support proposals can raise ethical and value issues for builders and managers. These issues must be addressed. The nine critical incident scenarios should stimulate discussion and analysis of decision support ethical issues. Project champions are important and they should anticipate and manage resistance to an innovative DSS. Choosing appropriate change strategies can increase the chances a project will be a success. The next generation of computerized decision support will be more powerful, more integrated in our lives and organizations, and more important to organization success and failure.

Notes

Chapter 1

1. Tversky and Kahneman (1974); Kahneman, Slovic, and Tversky (1982).
2. Power (2007, March 10). See http://dssresources.com/history/dsshistory.html
3. Land (2008); Frank Land responded by email to six questions from Dan Power.
4. Everett, Zraket, and Bennington (1957).
5. Davis (1974).
6. Morton (1967, 1971).
7. Gorry and Morton (1971, Fall).
8. Rockart (1979, March–April).
9. Alter (1975, 1980).
10. Sprague and Carlson (1982).
11. Gray (1983), p. 3.
12. DeSanctis and Gallupe (1987); Gray (1981); Huber (1984); Turoff and Hiltz (1982).
13. Nylund (1999, July).
14. Inmon (1991).
15. Codd, Codd, and Salley (1993); Dhar and Stein (1997); Pendse (1997).
16. Powell (2001, February).
17. Simon (1945). Expanded version with additional materials released in 1976.
18. Simon (1973).
19. Bohlen, Beal, and Rogers (1957).
20. Moore (1991).
21. Ventana Research.
22. McKinsey Global Institute.

Chapter 2

1. http://dssresources.com/glossary/48.php
2. Sprague and Carlson (1982), p. 9.
3. Glossary was at http://www.106.ibm.com/developerworks
4. Sprague (1980); Sprague and Carlson (1982).
5. Davenport and Harris (2007).
6. IDC is a global market intelligence firm, http://www.idc.com

7. See Note 3.
8. Imhoff (2007, February 28).
9. Aberdeen Group (2007, December).
10. Imhoff (2007, October 23).
11. Swift (2003, November 07).
12. Margulius (2002, January 17).
13. http://en.wikipedia.org/wiki/Business_Activity_Monitoring
14. Barclay and Murray (1997); Davenport and Prusak (1998); http://www.sveiby.com; Liang, OuYang, and Power (2007); Nonaka and Takeuchi (1995); Wiig (1997).
15. Barclay and Murray (1997).
16. Alavi and Leidner (2001), pp. 115, 119.
17. Wilson (2002).
18. Dugage (2005, December 1).
19. Houdeshel and Watson (1987, March); Rockart (1979); Rockart and Treacy (1982, January–February).
20. Kelly (1994, 2002).
21. Imhoff and White (2008, August 27).

Chapter 3

1. Alter (1980); Arnott and Pervan (2005); Holsapple and Whinston (1996).
2. Simon (1960).
3. Taylor and Raden (2007).
4. This framework originated in Power (2000, Fall; 2001, June 19–22; 2002, 2004, February; 2007, September 13).
5. Alter (1980).
6. Holsapple and Whinston (1996), pp. 144–145.
7. Turban and Aronson (1995).
8. Alter (1980); Watson, Rainer, and Koh (1991, March).
9. Codd, Codd, and Salley (1993).
10. Bush (1945, July).
11. Alter (1980); Klein and Methlie (1995).

Chapter 4

1. Finley (2011).
2. Inmon (1991, 2002).
3. Based on various sources and case studies.
4. cf., Anahory and Murray (1997), pp. 22–26.
5. Lohr (2011, April 23).

6. MacDonald (2005, August 12).
7. Norman and Thanisch (1999, September 8).
8. Whatis.com
9. Teradata Warehouse Technical Overview (2005, September).
10. Mahapatra and Mishra (2000, August).
11. Walter (2006).
12. http://www-01.ibm.com/software/data/netezza/
13. Vaughan (2008, June 30).
14. Samir Sakpal's Blog at http://www.frost.com/reg/blog-personal-index .do?userId=11343
15. Jain (2011, June).

Chapter 5

1. Davenport, Cohen, and Jacobson (2005, May).
2. Morris (2001, April).
3. Gemignani (2008, July 7).
4. Codd, Codd, and Salley (1993).
5. Pendse (2002, April 7).
6. IBM Analytics Quotient (AQ) quiz at http://www-01.ibm.com/software /analytics/aq/
7. Miller (2012, February 14).
8. Davenport, Cohen, and Jacobson (2005).
9. Power (2004).
10. Sprague and Carlson (1982).
11. Decisioneering Staff (2004, March 16); Palisade Staff (2001, May 22).
12. Durfee (2004, June 15); Murphy (2007); Raden (2005, February 26).
13. Microsoft help, http://office.microsoft.com/en-us/assistance/
14. Winston (2004).
15. Pannell (1997).
16. Eppen, Gould, and Schmidt (1993); Evan and Olson (2002).
17. Evans and Olson (2002).
18. Evans and Olson (2002).
19. Evans and Olson (2002), pp. 161–163.
20. Evans and Olson (2002), pp. 163–165.
21. Evans and Olson (2002), pp. 176–179.
22. Bonabeau (2002).
23. http://thesims.com
24. Roush (2007, July/August).
25. Stephenson (1992).
26. Chesher (1994, Fall).

27. Galouye (1964).
28. Galouye (1964), p. 83.
29. http://www.jaronlanier.com/general.html
30. Walker (1988, September 1).
31. McCosh and Scott Morton (1978).

Chapter 6

1. Davenport (2005, April 29).
2. Coakley (2001).
3. Porter and Millar (1985).
4. Porter (1979).
5. Kettinger, Grover, Guha, and Segars (1994).
6. Trull (1966).
7. Kerr and Jermier (1978).
8. Klein and Methlie (1995), pp. 172–181; Winograd and Flores (1986).
9. http://decisionautomation.com

Chapter 7

1. Stabell (1983), pp. 225–232.
2. Hammer and Champy (1993), p. 37.
3. Hammer and Champy (1993).
4. Hammer (1990).
5. Whitten, Bentley, and Barlow (1994).
6. http://asuret.com
7. Prahalad and Hamel (1990).

Chapter 8

1. This quotation has been attributed to Robert Stakes without citation, it is worth repeating.
2. Kotter (1979); Bennis et al. (1969).
3. http://www.gridcafe.org/what-is-the-grid.html
4. Kotter and Schlessinger (1979).
5. http://www.1keydata.com/datawarehousing/open-source-business-intelligence.html
6. http://dssresources.com/faq/index.php?action=artikel&id=147
7. http://www.metaversejournal.com/
8. http://www-01.ibm.com/software/data/bigdata/; Zikopoulos et al. (2013).

Glossary

Ad-Hoc Query: Any spontaneous or unplanned question or query. It is a query that consists of dynamically constructed SQL and is one capability in a data-driven DSS.

Aggregate Data: Structured data that results from applying a process to more detailed data—data that is summarized or averaged.

Alerts: A notification from an event that a trigger has exceeded a predefined threshold. Alerts are used with data-driven DSS.

Algorithm: A set of rules for calculating results or solving problems that have been programmed for use in a model-driven DSS.

Analytics: A broad term that includes quantitative analysis of data and building quantitative models. Analytics is the science of analysis and discovery. Analysis may process data from a data warehouse, may result in building model-driven DSS or may occur in a special study using statistical or data mining software. In general, analytics refers to quantitative analysis and manipulation of data.

Big Data: A term used to describe large sets of structured and unstructured data. Data sets are continually increasing in size and may grow too large for traditional storage and retrieval. Data may be captured and analyzed as it is created and then stored in files.

Business Activity Monitoring (BAM): BAM is a real-time version of business performance monitoring and operational BI and is a data-driven DSS.

Business Analytics: Application of analytical tools to business questions. Business Analytics focuses on developing insights and understanding related to business performance using quantitative and statistical methods. Business Analytics includes Business Intelligence and Reporting.

Business Intelligence: BI is a popularized, umbrella term that describes a set of concepts and methods used to improve business decision making by using fact-based support systems. The term is sometimes used interchangeably with briefing books and executive information systems. A Business Intelligence system is a data-driven DSS.

Business Process Management (BPM): Using a specialized information system to improve business processes such as planning and forecasting to help managers define, measure, and manage performance against strategic goals. Management translates goals into key performance indicators (KPIs) that are monitored using computerized systems. A computer-based dashboard is a BPM or corporate performance management (CPM) tool.

Business Rules: If-then statements of business policies and guidelines. Rules specify operations, definitions, and constraints. The rules are in a syntax that can be included in a computerized system and should be understandable to managers.

Client–server architecture: A network architecture in which computers on a network act as a server managing files and network services, or as a client where users run applications and access servers.

Cognitive Overload: A psychological phenomenon characterized by an excessive amount of information for a decision maker. The amount of information exceeds the person's cognitive capacity. DSS can reduce or increase cognitive overload.

Communications-Driven DSS: A decision support system that uses network and communications technologies to facilitate collaboration, communication, and decision making.

Computer Supported Special Study: Use of general purpose computer software tools like Excel or a data mining tool for analyzing specific questions that are nonroutine and unstructured.

Cost–Benefit Analysis: A tool used in decision support special studies that can assist in the allocation of capital. Cost–Benefit Analysis is a systematic, quantitative method for assessing the life cycle costs and benefits of competing alternatives. One identifies both tangible and intangible costs and benefits.

Cycle Time: The time interval required to complete a task or function. A cycle starts with the beginning of the first step in a process and ends with the completion of the final step.

Dashboard: A display of data in a simple visual format. A visualization tool that provides graphic depictions of current KPIs. Data displayed may be real time or historical.

Data: Atomic facts, text, graphics, images, sound, analog or digital live-video segments that are in a form that can be processed by a computer. Data is the raw material of an information system supplied by data producers and is used by managers and analysts to create information.

Data Mart: A focused collection of operational data that is usually confined to a specific aspect or subject of a business such as customers, products, or suppliers. It is a more focused decision support data store than a data warehouse.

Data Mining: A class of analytical applications that help users search for hidden patterns in a data set. Data mining is a process of analyzing large amounts of data to identify data–content relationships. Data mining is one tool used in decision support special studies. This process is also known as data surfing or knowledge discovery.

Data Visualization: Presenting data and summary information using graphics, animation, and three-dimensional displays. Tools for visually displaying information and relationships often using dynamic and interactive graphics.

Data Warehouse: A very large database designed to support decision making in organizations. It is usually batch updated and structured for rapid online queries and managerial summaries. A data warehouse is a subject-oriented, integrated, time-variant, nonvolatile collection of data.

Data-Driven DSS: A category or type of DSS that emphasizes access to and manipulation of a time series of internal company data and sometimes external data. Simple file systems accessed by query and retrieval tools provide the most elementary level of decision support functionality. Data warehouse systems often provide additional functionality. Analytical processing provides the highest level of functionality and decision support linked to analysis of large collections of historical data. Some data-driven DSS use real-time data to assist in operational performance monitoring.

Decision Automation: This broad term refers to computerized systems that make decisions and have some capability to independently act upon them. Decision automation refers to using technologies including computer processing to make decisions and implement programmed decision processes.

Decision Making Support: Using information technology to assist in one or more steps in the process of gathering and evaluating information about a situation, identifying a need for a decision, identifying or in other ways defining relevant alternative courses of action, choosing the "best," the "most appropriate," or the "optimum" action, and then applying the solution and choice in the situation.

Decision Scientist: A professional trained in quantitative and decision aiding tools and techniques. Decision scientists are experts in management science and database methods and tools. A decision scientist analyzes and implements computational rules related to business and organization activity. A decision scientist applies quantitative and behavioral methods to problems.

Decision Support: A broad, general concept that prescribes using computerized systems and other tools to assist in individual, group, and organization decision making.

Decision Support System (DSS): A DSS is an interactive computer-based system or subsystem intended to help decision makers use communications technologies, data, documents, knowledge or models, to identify and solve problems, complete decision process tasks, and make decisions.

Document-Driven DSS: A computerized support system that integrates a variety of storage and processing technologies to provide complete document retrieval and analysis to assist in decision making.

Drill Down/Up: An analytical technique that lets a DSS user navigate among levels of data ranging from the most summarized (up) to the most detailed (down).

Enterprise Decision Management (EDM): Automating operational decisions using business rules software with predictive analytics.

Enterprise-Wide DSS: A DSS that is broadly useful in an organization. It is usually a data-driven DSS that supports a large group of managers in a networked client–server environment with a specialized data warehouse as part of the DSS architecture.

Exception Reporting: A reporting philosophy and approach that involves only identifying unanticipated, abnormal, or anomalous information. Reports are designed to display significant exceptions in results and data. The idea is to "flag" important information and bring it quickly to the attention of a decision maker. Exception reporting can be implemented in any type of DSS, but it is particularly useful in data-driven DSS.

Executive Information Systems (EIS): A computerized system intended to provide current and appropriate information to support decision making for executives. EIS offer strong reporting and drill-down capabilities.

Explicit Knowledge: Knowledge that can be codified, such as plans, customer preferences, specifications, manuals, instructions for assembling components, and can be stored in a document-driven or knowledge-driven DSS.

Information: Data that has been processed to create meaning. Information is intended to expand the knowledge of the person who receives it. Information is the output of decision support and information systems.

Inter-Organizational DSS: A DSS that serves a company's organizational stakeholders including customers and suppliers.

Knowledge: A collection of specialized facts, procedures, and judgment rules. Knowledge refers to what one knows and understands. Knowledge is categorized as unstructured, structured, explicit, or implicit. What we know we know we call explicit knowledge. Knowledge that is unstructured and understood, but not clearly expressed, we call implicit knowledge.

Knowledge-Driven DSS: A type of DSS that can suggest or recommend actions to managers. These systems store and help users apply knowledge for a specific problem.

Knowledge Management (KM): Knowledge management promotes activities and processes to acquire, create, document, and share formal explicit knowledge and informal implicit knowledge. Knowledge management involves identifying a group of people who have a need to share knowledge, developing technological support that enables knowledge sharing, and creating a process for transferring and disseminating knowledge.

Knowledge Management System (KMS): KMS can store and manage information in a variety of electronic formats. The software may assist in knowledge capture, categorization, deployment, inquiry, discovery, or communication. Document-driven DSS and knowledge-driven DSS are Knowledge Management Systems.

Model-Driven DSS: A category or type of DSS that emphasizes access to and manipulation of algebraic, financial, optimization, or simulation models.

On-Line Analytical Processing (OLAP): OLAP is software for manipulating multidimensional data from a variety of sources that has been stored in a data warehouse. The software can create various views and representations of the data. OLAP software provides fast, consistent, interactive access to shared, multidimensional data.

Operational Business Intelligence: Operational BI provides time-sensitive, relevant information to operations managers and frontline, customer-facing employees to support daily work processes. These data-driven DSS differ from other DSS in terms of purpose, targeted users, data latency, data detail, and availability.

Predictive Analytics: A general term for using simple and complex models to predict what will happen to support decision making. A process of using a quantitative model and current real-time or historical data to generate a score that is predictive of future behavior. Statistical analysis of historical data identifies a predictive model to support a specific decision task.

Scenario Analysis: A scenario analysis involves changing parameters in a model and then examining the results. A tool that helps a user explore different scenarios by changing a range of input values.

Semistructured Decision Situation: Some factors related to a decision or choice are structured while others are unstructured. Only some factors are known and can be specified.

Sensitivity Analysis: An analysis that involves calculating a decision model multiple times with different inputs so a modeler can analyze the alternative results.

Specific Decision Support System: A computer-based system that has a narrow decision-making purpose. The system helps a person accomplish a particular decision-making task.

Structured Decision Situation: A routine or standardized decision where factors are identifiable and solution techniques are known and available. The structural elements in the situation, for example, alternatives, criteria, environmental variables, are known, defined, and understood. Results can be measured and the problem is amenable to quantitative analysis.

Unstructured Decision Situation: A complex set of factors and no standard solutions exist for resolving the situation. Some or all of the structural elements of the decision situation are undefined, ill-defined, or unknown. For example, goals may be poorly defined, alternatives may be incomplete or incomparable, choice criteria may be hard to measure or difficult to link to goals.

User Interface: A component of a computerized system that provides communication and interaction between a system and its user. This component is also called the dialogue component or human to computer interface. An interface is a set of commands or menus through which a user communicates with a program.

Virtual World: An immersive three-dimensional virtual space where one's avatar interacts with a computer-simulated world. Some people only associate virtual worlds with games, but such environments can be used for decision support.

What-If Analysis: The capability of "asking" the software package what the effect will be of changing some of the input data or independent variables.

References and Bibliography

Aberdeen Group. (2007, December). *Operational BI: Getting real time about performance*. Retrieved September 3, 2008, from https://www304.ibm.com /jct03004c/tools/cpeportal/fileserve/download0/140686/AberdeenOper ationBIperf.pdf?contentid=140686

Alavi, M., & Leidner, D. E. (2001, March). Knowledge management and knowledge management systems: Conceptual foundations and research issues. *MIS Quarterly 25*(1), 107–136.

Alter, S. L. (1975). *A study of computer aided decision making in organizations*. Unpublished doctoral dissertation, Massachusetts Institute of Technology.

Alter, S. L. (1980). *Decision support systems: Current practice and continuing challenge*. Reading, MA: Addison-Wesley.

Anahory, S., & D. Murray (1997). *Data Warehousing in the Real World: A Practical Guide for Building Decision Support Systems*. Reading, MA: Addison-Wesley.

Arnott, D., & Pervan, G. (2005). A critical analysis of decision support systems research. *Journal of Information Technology 20*(2), 67–87.

Barclay, R. O., & Murray, P. C. (1997). What is knowledge management? *Knowledge Praxis*. Retrieved May 13, 2009, from http://www.media-access .com/whatis.html

Beal, G. M., Rogers, E. M., & Bohlen, J. M. (1957). Validity of the concept of stages in the adoption process. *Rural Sociology 22*(2),166–168.

Bennis, W., Benne, K. D., & Chin, R. (Eds.). (1969). *The planning of change* (2nd ed.). New York, NY: Holt, Rinehart and Winston.

Bonabeau, E. (2002). Agent-based modeling: Methods and techniques for simulating human systems. *Proceedings of the National Academy of Sciences of the United States of America, 99*(10), 7280–7287.

Bush, V. (1945, July). As we may think. *Atlantic Monthly*. Retrieved July 13, 2009, from http://www.theatlantic.com/doc/194507/bush

Chesher, C. (1994, Fall). Colonizing virtual reality: Construction of the discourse of virtual reality, 1984–1992. *Cultronix 1*(1). Retrieved September 9, 2012, from http://cultronix.eserver.org/chesher/

Coakley, T. (2001, April 24). Decision superiority: A junior officer's practical guide to knowledge-based operations. *Air & Space Power Journal*. Approved for public release at http://www.airpower.maxwell.af.mil/airchronicles/cc /coakley.html

Codd, E. F., Codd, S. B., & Salley, C. T. (1993). *Providing OLAP (On-line analytical processing) to user-analysts: An IT mandate.* E. F. Codd and Associates (sponsored by Arbor Software Corporation).

Davis, G. (1974). *Management information systems: Conceptual foundations, structure, and development.* New York, NY: McGraw-Hill.

Davenport, T. H. (2005, April 29). Executives see business intelligence emerging as crucial competitive advantage. DMReview.com Online News. Retrieved April 29, 2005, from http://www.dmreview.com/article_sub.cfm?articleId=1026818

Davenport, T., Cohen, D., & Jacobson, A. (2005, May). Competing on analytics. Babson, MA: Working Knowledge Research Center. Retrieved September 9, 2012, from http://www.babsonknowledge.org/analytics.pdf

Davenport, T. H., & Harris, J. G. (2007). *Competing on analytics: The new science of winning.* Harvard Business School Press.

Davenport, T. H., & Prusak, L. (1998). *Working knowledge: How organizations manage what they know.* Boston, MA: Harvard Business School Press.

Decisioneering Staff (2001, March 16). SunTrust 'Banks' on Crystal Ball for assessing the risk of commercial loans. Decisioneering, Inc., November 1998, posted at DSSResources.COM

DeSanctis, G., & Gallupe, R. B. (1987, May). A foundation for the study of group decision support systems. *Management Science 33*(5), 589–609.

Dhar, V., & Stein, R. (1997). *Intelligent decision support methods: The science of knowledge.* Upper Saddle River, NJ: Prentice Hall.

Dugage, M. (2005, December 1). KM programs are dead. Long live KM! Retrieved July 13, 2009, from http://blog.mopsos.com

Durfee, D. (2004, June 15). Spreadsheet hell. *CFO Magazine*, Retrieved September 9, 2012, from http://www.cfo.com/article.cfm/3014451

Eppen, G. D., Gould, F. J., & Schmidt, C. P. (1993). *Introductory management science* (4th ed.). EnglewoodCliffs, NJ: Prentice Hall.

Evans, J. R., & Olson, D. L. (2002). *Introduction to simulation and risk analysis* (2nd ed.). Upper Saddle River, NJ: Prentice Hall.

Everett, R. R., Zraket, C. A., & Bennington, H. D. (1957). Sage: A data processing system for air defense MITRE. *Proceedings of EJCC*, 148–155. Retrieved September 9, 2012, from http://ed-thelen.org/sage.html

Finley, K. (2011, January 6). Business analytics predictions from Gartner and Forrester. ReadWriteWeb. Retrieved September 9, 2012, from http://www.readwriteweb.com/enterprise/2011/01/business-analytics-predictions.php

Galouye, D. F. (1964). *Simulacron-3.* New York, NY: Bantam Books.

Gemignani, Z. (2008, July 7). Why analytical applications fail. Retrieved September 9, 2012, from http://www.juiceanalytics.com/writing/why-analytical-applications-fail/

Gorry, A., & Scott Morton, M. S. (1971, Fall). A framework for information systems. *Sloan Management Review 13*(1), 56–79.

Gray, P. (1983). *Guide to IFPS (interactive financial planning system)*. New York, NY: McGraw-Hill.

Gray, P., Berry, N. W., Aronofsky, J., Helmer, O., Kane, G. R., & Perkins, T. E. (1981). The SMU decision room project. *Transactions of the 1st international conference on decision support systems: DSS-81* (pp. 122–129). Atlanta, GA.

Hammer, M. (1990, July–August). Reengineering work: Don't automate, obliterate. *Harvard Business Review 68*(4), 104–112.

Hammer, M., & Champy, J. A. (1993). *Reengineering the corporation: A manifesto for business revolution*. New York, NY: Harper Business Books.

Holsapple, C., & Whinston, A. (1996). *Decision support systems: A knowledge based approach*. Minneapolis, MN: West Publishing.

Houdeshel, G., & Watson, H. (1987, March). The management information and decision support (MIDS) system at Lockheed-Georgia. *MIS Quarterly 11*(1), 127–140.

Huber, G. P. (1984). Issues in the design of group decision support systems. *MIS Quarterly 8*(3), 195–204.

Imhoff, C. (2007, February 28). Enterprise architectures for BI and data-driven decision support. Interviewed by Daniel J. Power. Retrieved December 27, 2012, from http://dssresources.com/interviews/imhoff/imhoff2282007.html

Imhoff, C. (2007, October 23). *Operational business intelligence—a prescription for operational success*. Retrieved September 3, 2008, from http://www.b-eye -network.com/view/6281

Imhoff, C., & White, C. (2008, August 27). Full circle: Decision intelligence (DSS 2.0). Retrieved May 5, 2009, from http://www.b-eye-network.com /view/8385

Inmon, W. H. (1991). *Third wave processing: Database machines and decision support systems*. Wellesley, MA: QED Information Sciences.

Inmon, W. (2002, March 15). *Building the Data Warehouse* (3rd edn), Wiley.

Jain, M. (2011, June). Surveying the mobile BI landscape. *Digital Software Magazine*. Retrieved September 9, 2012, from http://www.softwaremag .com/focus-areas/business-intelligence/commentary/surveying-the-mobile -bi-landscape/

Kahneman, D., Slovic, P., & Tversky, A. (Eds.). (1982). *Judgment under uncertainty: Heuristics and biases*. Cambridge, UK: Cambridge University Press.

Kelly, F. (1994, October). Implementing an executive information system (EIS). Retrieved September 9, 2012, from http://dssresources.com/subscriber/pass word/papers/features/kelly11072002.html

Kelly, F. (2002). Implementing an Executive Information System (EIS). DSS Resources.COM, 11/07/2002, HTML File. This is a review paper from 1994 that was featured at ceoreview.com

Kerr, S., & Jermier, J. M. (1978). Substitutes for leadership: Their meaning and measurement. *Organizational Behavior and Human Performance 22*, 375–403.

Kettinger, W., Grover, V., Guha, S., & Segars, A. (1994). Strategic information systems revisited. *MIS Quarterly 18*(1), 31–58.

Klein, M., & Methlie, L. B. (1995). *Knowledge-based decision support systems with applications in business.* Chichester, UK: Wiley.

Kotter, J. P., & Schlesinger, L. A. (1979). Choosing strategies for change. *Harvard Business Review 57*, 106–114.

Land, F. (2008, March 16). Frank Land's reflections. Retrieved September 9, 2012, from http://dssresources.com/reflections/land/land03162008.html

Liang, T.-P., OuYang, Y. C., & Power, D. J. (2007). Effects of knowledge management capabilities on perceived performance: An empirical examination. In U. Kulkarni, D. J. Power, & R. Sharda (Eds.), *Annals of information systems, Vol. 2: Decision support for global enterprises* (pp. 139–163). New York, NY: Springer.

Lohr, S. (2011, April 23). When there's no such thing as too much information. *New York Times.*

MacDonald, M. (2005, August 12), What is a pivot table, Excel: The missing manual. Retrieved September 9, 2012, from http://oreilly.com/windows/archive/whatisapivottable.html

McCosh, A., & Scott Morton, M. S. (1978) *Management decision support systems.* London, UK: Macmillan Press.

Mahapatra, T., & Mishra, S. (2000, August). *Oracle parallel processing.* O'Reilly. Retrieved September 9, 2012, from http://www.oreilly.com/catalog/oraclepp/chapter/ch01.html

Margulius, D. L. (2002, January 17). Dawn of the real-time enterprise. *Infoworld.* Retrieved September 9, 2012 from http://www.infoworld.com/t/platforms/dawn-real-time-enterprise-726

McKinsey Global Institute. Michigan State University to introduce students to analytics and big data using IBM Watson. Retrieved from http://dssresources.com/news/3590.php

Merrill, M. (2009, April 15). Decision support system aids military during patient transfers. *Healthcare IT News.* Retrieved September 9, 2012, from http://www.healthcareitnews.com/news/decision-support-system-aids-military-during-patient-transfers

Miller, S. (2012, February 14). Analytics: The widening divide. Retrieved September 9, 2012, from http://www.information-management.com/blogs/analytics-EMC-MIT-data-science-BI-10021944-1.html?ET=information mgmt:e2971:2078848a:&st=email&utm_source=editorial&utm_medium=email&utm_campaign=IM_Blogs_021512

Moore, G. A. (1991). *Crossing the Chasm.* New York, NY: Harper Business.

Morris, H. (2001, April). Trends in analytic applications. DM Review.

Murphy, S. (2007). Spreadsheet hell. Proceedings of the European Spreadsheet Risks International Group. pp. 15–20 at http://arxiv.org/abs/0801.3118

Nonaka, I., & Takeuchi, H. (1995). *The knowledge-creating company: How Japanese companies create the dynamics of innovation*. New York, NY: Oxford University Press.

Norman, M. G., & Thanisch, P. (1999, September 8). Parallel database technology: An evaluation and comparison of scalable systems. Bloor Research Group. Retrieved September 9, 2012, from http://www.dpu.se/blopdt_e.html

Nylund, A. (1999, July). Tracing the BI family tree. *Knowledge Management*.

Oracle. (2009, May 6). Collaborate 2009. Press release. Retrieved from http://dss resources.com/news/2802.php

Palisade Staff (2001, May 22). Procter & Gamble Uses @RISK and PrecisionTree World-Wide. Palisade Corp., Spring 2001, posted at DSSResources.COM

Pannell, D. J. (1997). Sensitivity analysis of normative economic models: Theoretical framework and practical strategies. *Agricultural Economics 16*, 139–152, at http://cyllene.uwa.edu.au/~dpannell/dpap971f.htm

Pendse, N. (1997). Origins of today's OLAP products. *The OLAP Report*. Retrieved from http://www.olapreport.com

Pendse, N. (2002, April 7). What is OLAP? DSSResources.COM, Retrieved September 9, 2012, from http://dssresources.com/subscriber/password/papers/features/pendse04072002.htm

Porter, M. E. (1979, March–April). How competitive forces shape strategy. *Harvard Business Review 57*(2), 137–145.

Porter, M. E., & Millar, V. E. (1985, July–August). How information gives you competitive advantage. *Harvard Business Review 63*(4), 149–161.

Powell, R. (2001, February). *DM Review*: A 10 year journey. *DM Review*. Retrieved March 10, 2001, from http://www.dmreview.com

Power, D. J. (2000, Fall). *Decision support systems hyperbook*. Cedar Falls, IA: DSSResources.COM. Retrieved September 9, 2012, from http://dssresources.com/dssbook

Power, D. J. (2001, June 19–22). Supporting decision-makers: An expanded framework. In A. Harriger (Ed.), *Proceedings of 2001 Informing Science Conference* (pp. 431–436). Krakow, Poland: Cracow University of Economics.

Power, D. J. (2002). *Decision support systems: Concepts and resources for managers*. Westport, CT: Greenwood/Quorum Books.

Power, D. J. (2004, February). Specifying an expanded framework for classifying and describing decision support systems. *Communications of the Association for Information Systems 13*, 158–166.

Power, D. J. (2004, August 30). A Brief History of Spreadsheets. Retrieved September 9, 2012, from http://dssresources.com/history/sshistory.html, version 3.6, 08/30/2004.

Power, D. J. (2007, March 10). A brief history of decision support systems. Retrieved September 9, 2012, from http://DSSResources.COM/history/dss history.html

Power, D. J. (2007, September 13). A framework for understanding computerized decision support. *Bill Inmon eNewsletter*. Business Intelligence Network.

Prahalad, C. K., & Hamel, G. (1990). The core competence of the corporation. *Harvard Business Review 68*(3), 79–91.

Raden, N. (2005, February 26). Shedding light on shadow IT: Is Excel running your business? DSSResources.COM, at http://dssresources.com/papers/features/raden/raden02262005.html

Rockart, J. F. (1979, March–April). Chief executives define their own data needs. *Harvard Business Review 57*(2), 81–93.

Rockart, J. F., & Treacy, M. E. (1982, January–February). The CEO goes online. *Harvard Business Review 60*(1), 82–88.

Roush, W. (2007, July/August). Second Earth. *MIT Technology Review*, 38–48, http://www.technologyreview.com/Infotech/18911/page1/

Scott Morton, M. S. (1967). *Computer-driven visual display devices—their impact on the management decision-making process*. Unpublished doctoral dissertation, Harvard Business School.

Scott Morton, M. S. (1971). *Management decision systems: Computer-based support for decision making*. Boston, MA: Division of Research, Graduate School of Business Administration, Harvard University.

Simon, H. A. (1945). *Administrative behavior: A study of decision-making processes in administrative organization* (3rd ed.). New York, NY: Free Press.

Simon, H. A. (1960). *The new science of management decision*. New York, NY: Harper & Row.

Simon, H. A. (1973). Applying information technology to organization design. *Public Administration Review 33*, 268–278.

Sprague, R. H., Jr. (1980, December). A framework for the development of decision support systems. *Management Information Systems Quarterly 4*(4), 1–26.

Sprague, R. H., Jr., & Carlson, E. D. (1982). *Building effective decision support systems*. Englewood Cliffs, NJ: Prentice Hall.

Stabell, C. B. (1983). A decision-oriented approach to building DSS. In J. L. Bennett (Ed.), *Building decision support systems* (pp. 221–260). Reading, MA: Addison-Wesley.

Stephenson, N. (1992). *Snow crash*. New York, NY: Bantam Books.

Swift, R. (2003, November 7). *Comments on decision support and CRM*. Interviewed by Daniel J. Power. Retrieved May 12, 2009, from http://dssresources.com/interviews/swift/swift11072003.html

Taylor, J., & Raden, N. (2007). *Smart enough systems: How to deliver competitive advantage by automating hidden decisions*. Englewood Cliffs, NJ: Prentice Hall PTR.

Teradata Warehouse Technical Overview (2005, September). Teradata Pioneered Data Warehousing. EB-3025, Retrieved September 9, 2012, from http://www.teradata.com/t/pdf.aspx?a=83673&b=84876

Trull, S. G. (1966, February). Some factors involved in determining total decision success. *Management Science 12*(6), B-270–B-280.

Turban, E., & Aronson, J. E. (1995). *Decision support and intelligent systems* (4th ed.). Upper Saddle River, NJ: Prentice Hall.

Turoff, M., & Hiltz, S. R. (1982). Computer support for group versus individual decisions. *IEEE Transactions on Communications 30*(1), 82–90.

Tversky, A., & Kahneman, D. (1974). Judgment under uncertainty: Heuristics and biases. *Science 185*, 1124–1131.

Vaughan, S. (2008, June 30). Intelligence on the go: Mobile delivery of BI. *Dashboard Insight*. Retrieved September 9, 2012, from http://www .dashboardinsight.com/articles/new-concepts-in-business-intelligence /intelligence-on-the-go.aspx?page=4

Ventana Research. Five causes of information management immaturity. Retrieved from http://www.information-management.com/gallery/IM-Ven tana-governance-big-data-analytics-DM-ROI-10022546-1.html?ET=infor mationmgmt:e3246:207884

Walker, J. (1988, September 1). Through the looking glass. Retrieved September 9, 2012, from http://www.fourmilab.ch/autofile/www/chapter2_69.html

Walter, T. (2006). Scalability, performance, availability. *Teradata Magazine Online*. Retrieved April 9, 2006, from http://www.teradata.com/t/go.aspx /index.html?id=115886

Watson, H. J., Rainer, R. K., & Koh, C. (1991, March). Executive information systems: A framework for development and a survey of current practices. *MIS Quarterly 15*(1), 13–30.

Whitten, J. L., Bentley, L. D., & Barlow, V. M. (1994). *Systems analysis and design methods* (3rd ed.). Burr Ridge, IL: Irwin.

Wiig, K. (1997). Knowledge management: Where did it come from, and where will it go? *Journal of Expert Systems With Applications 13*(1), 1–14.

Wilson, T. D. (2002). The nonsense of "knowledge management" (Paper no. 144). *Information Research 8*(1). Retrieved May 12, 2009, from http://Inform ationR.net/ir/8-1/paper144.html

Winograd, T., & Flores, F. (1986). *Understanding computers and cognition*. Reading, MA: Addison-Wesley.

Winston, W. L. (2004). *Microsoft Excel data analysis and business modeling*. Microsoft Press.

Zikopoulos, P., D. deRoos, K. Parasuraman, T. Deutsch, D. Corrigan, J. Giles (2013). *Harness the Power of Big Data*. New York: McGraw Hill.

Index

A

Aberdeen Group, 22
Activity-scanning simulation, 87, 88
Ad hoc data filtering and retrieval, 42
Ad hoc search and retrieval, 44
Administrative Behavior (Simon), 12
Adoption, of DSS, 13–14
Advisory systems, 45
Agenda creation, 41
Agent-based and multiagent
    simulation, 87, 89, 94
Alerts and triggers, 42
AMPP. *See* Asymmetric massively
    parallel processing
Analytical processing, 76
Analytic applications, 76–77
Analytics, 53, 73. *See also* Business
    intelligence (BI); Decision
    support system (DSS)
    applications, 76–77
    defined, 20
    mobile, 72
    processing, 76
    reporting, 20, 29, 73, 78
    simple, 68
Analytics quotient (AQ), 80
Ancillary, 39
Android, 71
Application and document sharing, 41
*Applying Information Technology to
    Organization Design* (Simon),
    12–13
AQ. *See* Analytics quotient
Asymmetric massively parallel
    processing (AMPP), 71
Atlantic Monthly (Bush), 43
Audit, decision process, 115–117
Autodesk, 90, 91

B

Backtrack capability, 46
BAM. *See* Business activity
    monitoring

BI. *See* Business intelligence
BI tools, 135
Biases, 3
Big data, 14, 66, 68, 74, 135
Blackberry, 71
Bloor Research Group, 69
BPI. *See* Business process intelligence
BPM. *See* Business performance
    management
Browsing and document
    navigation, 44
Builder prospective, analysis
    from, 130
*Building Effective Decision Support
    Systems,* 10
Business activity monitoring (BAM),
    24–25
Business intelligence (BI). *See also*
    Analytics; Decision support
    system
    data-driven DSS and, 53–74
    defined, 21–22
    mobile, 71–72
    operational, 22–24
    spreadsheets, 82–83
    reports, 56–59
Business intelligence systems, 19,
    35, 83
Business intelligence tools, 21, 77
Business performance management
    (BPM), 24–25
Business process intelligence (BPI), 25

C

C++, 71
Certainty information, 46
Change management, 133
Characteristics, of DSS, 38–39
Cigna, 103
Cloud computing, 135
Clustering, 78
CMS. *See* Content management
    system

Commercial data sources, 65
Communications-driven DSS, 35
    features of, 40–41
Competitive advantage, by decision
        support, 100–104
    cost advantage, 102
    customer segment needs, 103
    data warehouse, 100
    differentiation advantage, 102–103
Computer-aided design, 90
Computerized decision support
    basic characteristics of, 39
    benefits and advantages of, 98–100
    developing effective, 119
    first generation, 7–9
    history of, 7–11
    second generation, 9–10
    substitutes for, 105–110
    theory of, 11–13
    third generation, 10–11
    users, 5–7
Computer-supported special study,
        33–34
Concepts, DSS, 17–30
Consultation systems, 45
Content management system (CMS),
        43–44
Corporate performance management
        (CPM), 24
CPM. See Corporate performance
        management
Crossing the Chasm (Moore), 13
Cross tabulation, 78
Crystal Ball, 82
Crystal Reports, 4
Current possibilities, decision support
        system (DSS), 32
Customer/Stakeholder surveys and
        questionnaires, 65

D
DaimlerChrysler, 84
Database management system
        (DBMS), 55, 82
Data capture, 65
Data display, creating, 42
Data-driven DSS, 35
    business intelligence and, 53–74
    enterprise-wide, 62–64

    features of, 43–45
    parallel database technology for,
        69–70
    pivot tables in, 67–69
    sources for building, 64–66
Data-driven simulation, 87
Data extraction software. See ETL
        (extract, transform, and load)
Data management and
        summarization, 42
Data mart, 54. See also Data warehouse
Data quality, 80
Data retrieving, for specific case, 47
Data scientists, 68
Data sets, 20, 29, 66, 68, 73, 82–84
Data warehouse (DW), 54–55
    competitive advantage, 100
Data warehouse appliance, 70–71
DBMS. See Database management
        system
Decision automation
    defined, 32–33
Decision impact, 39
Decision-making
    biases, 3
Decision outcomes
    DSS impact on, 104–105
Decision process audit, 115–117
Decision quality, 3, 98, 104, 107,
        119, 131
Decision support feasibility study,
        119–121
Decision support opportunities,
        113–126
Decision support planning, 113–115
Decision support queries, 59–60
    SQL knowledge, by managers,
        61–62
Decision support system (DSS).
        See also Analytics; Business
        intelligence (BI)
    adoption of, 13–14
    advantages, 110
    air traffic monitoring, 6
    American Airlines, 6
    and reengineering, 117–119
    benefits of, 97–100
    characteristics of, 38–39
    concept map, 29

cost advantage, 102
current possibilities, 32
customer segment needs, 103
dairyman's cooperative, 6
defined, 18–20
differentiation advantage, 102–103
disadvantages, 110–112
ethical issues, 128–132
executives need for specialized,
    27–29
first generation, 7–9
for shipscheduling decisions, 5–6
framework, 37
Group Health Cooperative, 6
history timeline, 8
impact on decision outcomes,
    104–105
misuse of, 131
need for, 2–4
next-generation in, 134–135
planning, 113–115
required skills and knowledge by
    managers, 4–5
Siemens Solar Industries, 6
specific classification of, 49, 50
spectrum, 32, 34
spreadsheet-based, 81–83
Turban and Aronson, 6
types of, 34–37
US Coast Guard, 6
Decision support technology, 7, 14,
    108, 115
Direct observation, 65
Display confidence, 46
Documentation, 80
Document-driven DSS, 35
    features of, 43–45
Document management, 44
DSSResources.COM, 6, 7, 18, 82–83
DSS. See Decision support system
DW. See Data warehouse

E
EDBPM. See Event-driven business
    process management
EDM. See Enterprise decision
    management
EDW. See Enterprise data warehouse
    (EDW)

Enterprise data warehouse (EDW), 67
Enterprise decision management
    (EDM), 33
Enterprise-Wide, Data-Driven DSS,
    62–64
    steps to build, 63
EISs. See Executive information
    systems
Error analysis. See Specific types
Ethical issues, 128–132
ETL (extract, transform, and load)
    defined, 66
    and model-driven DSS, 83–84
    relation with BI and decision
        support, 66–67
Evaluation, 127–128. See also
    Formative evaluation;
    Summative evaluation
Event-driven business process
    management (EDBPM), 25
Event-driven simulation, 87, 88
Executive information systems (EISs),
    10, 17, 27–29, 31, 42, 53
Executives, and DSS, 27–29

F
Facilitation, 39
Fact-based analysis, 101
Feasibility study, 119–121
Fico.com, 6
Financial feasibility, 120–121
First generation decision support, 7–9
Formative evaluation, 127–128

G
GADS. See Geodata analysis and
    display system
Gap analysis. See SWOT (strengths,
    weaknesses, opportunities, and
    threats) analysis
GDSS. See Group decision support
    systems
Geodata analysis and display system
    (GADS), 5
Global positioning technology, 135
Goal seeking, 48, 78
Good decisions, 104
Good decision support software, 3
Google products, 4

Government data sources, 65
Grid computing, 15, 134
Group decision support systems
    (GDSS), 35, 40

H
Hadoop, 71
Historical Data Values, extracting, 48
How and why, explained, 46

I
IBM/ Cognos, 21
Identifiable, 39
Implementation risk, 122–124
Initiate actions, 46
Interaction, 39, 41
Intra-query parallelism, 70
Intrinsic Value per Share Calculator, 84
iPhone/iPad, 71
IS/IT staff, 55, 57, 125

J
Java, 71

K
Key performance indicators (KPIs),
    24, 57
KM. *See* Knowledge management
KMS. *See* Knowledge management
    systems
Knowledge-based systems, 45
Knowledge-driven DSS, 35–36. *See also*
    Advisory systems; Consultation
    systems; Knowledge-based
    systems, Recommender systems;
    Management expert systems;
    Rule-based DSS; Suggestion
    systems
features of, 45–47
Knowledge management (KM)
    defined, 25–27
Knowledge management systems
    (KMS), 26
KPIs. *See* Key performance indicators

L
LEO I. *See* Lyons Electronic Office I
Lyons Electronic Office I (LEO I), 7
Lyons Tea Shops, 7

M
Management expert systems, 45
Management information system
    (MIS), 9
Management of information, 25
Management of people, 25
Managerial perspective, analysis from,
    130–131
Managers
    IT knowledge, 4–5
    skills and knowledge required from,
    4–5
    SQL knowledge, for DSS, 61–62
MapReduce, 71
Matrix, The (movie), 90
Microsoft Excel, 82
Microsoft Office, 4
MicroStrategy, 21, 72
Mirror world, 90
Misuse, decision support data, 131
Mobile business intelligence, 71–72
Model-Driven DSS
    ETL software and, 83–84
    features of, 47–49
    predictive analytics and, 75–95
    rules for building successful,
    91–93
Modern decision support, 1–16
Monte Carlo simulation, 85, 87, 88
MIS. *See* Management information
    system
Multiple scenarios. *See* Multivariable
    analyses
Multiuser visual simulations, 90–91
Multivariable analyses, 78

N
Neuromancer (Gibson), 90
New system
    adaptive/incremental
        strategy, 133
    coercive strategy, 133
    education strategy, 133
    rational argument strategy, 133
    reducing resistance to, 132–134
Next-generation, DSS, 134–135
NLS. *See* oNLine System
North American Aerospace Defense
    Command, 7

O
OLAP. *See* On-Line Analytical
    Processing
On-Line Analytical Processing
    (OLAP), 11, 18, 22, 42, 54–55,
    73, 77–78
oNLine System (NLS), 9
Operational Business Intelligence,
    22–24
    application areas for, 23
    types of, 22–23
Oracle exadata database machine, 71
Oracle exadata storage servers, 71
Output selection, 48
Outsourcing, 124–126

P
Parallel database technology, 69–70
Parallelism, 15, 135
Passive electronic data
    capture, 65–66
Pine Cone Systems, 11
Pivot tables, 67–69
Polls, 41
Portable document format (PDF),
    56–57
Predefined data display, viewing, 43
Prediction, 80
Predictive analytics, 6–7
    developing, 79
    importance of, 79–81
    and model-driven DSS, 75–95
    in support of decision making,
        79–81
Premium Solver, 82
Privacy, 130
Probabilistic simulation, 87, 88
Process-based model simulation, 87
Production reports, 43
Project champions, 132–134
Project scope, 122–124
Project structure, 122–123
PushBI mobile business intelligence, 72
Python models, 71

Q
Queries, decision support, 59–60
Questions, asking, 46
Quicken.com, 84

R
RDBMS. *See* Relational database
    management systems
Real-time simulation, 87
Recommender systems, 45
Record meetings, 41
Red Brick Systems, 11
Reengineering, 117–119
@Risk, 82
Regression, 78
Relational database management
    systems (RDBMS), 59
Repeated use, 39
Reporting analytics, 20, 29, 73, 78
Report writing, 57–59
Resistance, to new system, 132–134
Risk, implementation, 122–123
Roller Coaster Tycoon (games), 91
Rule-based DSS, 45

S
SAGE. *See* Semi-automatic ground
    environment
SAP/Business Objects, 21
Scenario, creating and managing, 48
Scope, project, 122–124
SDLC. *See* Systems development life
    cycle (SDLC)
Second Earth (Roush), 90
Second generation decision support,
    9–10
Semi-automatic ground environment
    (SAGE), 7, 9, 16
Sensitivity analysis
    and "What If?" analysis, 84–87
SimCity (games), 89
SimCoaster (games), 89
Sims, The (games), 89
Simulacron-3 (Galouye), 90–91
Simulation
    and decision support, 87–89
Smart phone, 3–4, 17
Snow Crash (Stephenson), 90
Specialized DSS, and executives,
    27–29
Spreadsheet-based DSS, 81–83
SQL. *See* Structured query language
    (SQL)
Stream computing software, 135

Structured query language (SQL), 21, 59–62, 71
  AVG(), SUM(), and COUNT() key words, 61
  data field, retrieving, 61
  DISTINCT keyword, 61
  GROUP BY and HAVING key words, 62
  joining queries, 62
  FROM keyword, 61
  managers knowledge, 61–62
  nested queries, 62
  ORDER BY key word, 61
  SELECT key word, 60, 61
  WHERE key word, 61
Structure, project, 122–123
Substitutes, for computerized decision support, 105–110
  calculating a solution, 109
  checklist, 109
  face-to-face meetings, 109
  formalization, 109
  lessons from, 109–110
  paper-based filing cabinets, 109
Suggestion systems, 45
Summarization, 44, 78
Summative evaluation, 127–128
SUSE® Linux operating system, 71
SWOT (strengths, weaknesses, opportunities, and threats) analysis, 113
System Dynamics Group, 9
Systems development life cycle (SDLC), 62, 63

T
Tablet PC, 4, 46, 71–72
Task oriented, 39
Technical feasibility, 120
Teradata Data Warehouse Appliance, 71

Teradata Inc., 70
Text Mining and text analysis, 44
Third generation decision support, 10–11
Thirteenth Floor, The (movie), 90
Through the Looking Glass (Walker), 91
Time-dependent simulation, 87, 88
Trade-offs
  of outsourcing enterprise-wide DSS, 124–126
Traditional mathematical simulation, 87
Transaction data, 66
Trends in Analytic Applications (Morris), 76
Type I error, analysis, 68
Type II error, analysis, 68
Type III error, analysis, 68

V
Value elicitation, 48–49
Video conferencing, 40–41
Virtual reality (VR), 90–91
Virtual Reality Center, 84
Virtual world technologies, 135
Visual simulation, 87, 89
VPL, 90
VR. *See* Virtual reality (VR)

W
Web 2.0, 135
"What If?" analysis, 48
  limitations of, 86
  and sensitivity analysis, 84–87
Windows Mobile operating systems, 72
Writing reports, 57–59

Y
YouTube, 72

List of Questions With Links to Answers

1. Are BAM and BPM Decision Support Systems? p. 24, Chapter 2.
2. Can Decision Support Provide a Competitive Advantage? p. 100, Chapter 6.
3. Can DSS Impact Decision Outcomes? p. 104, Chapter 6.
4. Can Multi-User Visual Simulations Provide Real World Decision Support? p. 90, Chapter 5.
5. Can Project Champions Reduce Resistance to a New System? p. 132, Chapter 8.
6. Do Executives Need Specialized Decision Support? p. 27, Chapter 2.
7. How Can Simulation Be Used for Decision Support? p. 87, Chapter 5.
8. How Does Predictive Analytics Support Decision Making? p. 79, Chapter 5.
9. How Does Sensitivity Analysis Differ from "What If?" Analysis? p. 84, Chapter 5.
10. How Important Are Pivot Tables in Data-Driven Decision Support? p. 67, Chapter 4.
11. Is ETL Software Needed to Build a Model-Driven DSS? p. 83, Chapter 5.
12. Is Parallel Database Technology Needed for Data-Driven DSS? p. 69, Chapter 4.
13. Is Reengineering Necessary to Build an Effective DSS? p. 117, Chapter 7.
14. What Are Analytic Applications? p. 76, Chapter 5.
15. What Are Best Practices for BI Reports? p. 56, Chapter 4.
16. What Are Current Decision Support Possibilities? p. 32, Chapter 3.
17. What Are Ethical Issues Associated with Building and Using DSS? p. 128, Chapter 8.
18. What Are Examples of Routine Decision Support Queries? p. 59, Chapter 4.

19. What Are Potential Benefits of Decision Support? p. 97, Chapter 6.

20. What Are Sources of Data for Building a Data-Driven DSS? p. 64, Chapter 4.

21. What Are Substitutes for Computerized Decision Support? p. 105, Chapter 6.

22. What Are the Basic Characteristics of a Decision Support System? p. 38, Chapter 3.

23. What Are the Different Types of DSS? p. 34, Chapter 3.

24. What Are the Features of a Communications-Driven DSS? p. 40, Chapter 3.

25. What Are the Features of a Data-Driven DSS? p. 42, Chapter 3.

26. What Are the Features of a Document-Driven DSS? p. 43, Chapter 3.

27. What Are the Features of a Knowledge-Driven DSS? p. 45, Chapter 3.

28. What Are the Features of a Model-Driven DSS? p. 47, Chapter 3.

29. What Are the Possible Disadvantages of Building and Using DSS? p. 110, Chapter 6.

30. What Are the Rules for Building a Successful Model-Driven DSS? p. 91, Chapter 5.

31. What Are the Trade-Offs of Outsourcing Enterprise-Wide DSS? p. 124, Chapter 7.

32. What DSS Skills and Knowledge Do Managers Need? p. 4, Chapter 1.

33. What Factors Influence DSS Implementation Risk? p. 122, Chapter 7.

34. What Influences Adoption of Decision Support? p. 13, Chapter 1.

35. What Is a Computer-Supported Special Study? p. 33, Chapter 3.

36. What Is a Data Warehouse Appliance? p. 70, Chapter 4.

37. What Is a Decision Process Audit? p. 115, Chapter 7.

38. What Is a Decision Support Feasibility Study? p. 119, Chapter 7.

39. What Is a Decision Support System? p. 18, Chapter 2.

40. What Is Analytical Processing? p. 77, Chapter 5.

41. What Is Analytics? p. 20, Chapter 2.

42. What Is a Spreadsheet-Based DSS? p. 81, Chapter 5.

43. What Is Business Intelligence? p. 21, Chapter 2.

44. What Is Data Warehousing? p. 54, Chapter 4.

45. What Is Decision Automation? p. 32, Chapter 3.

46. What Is Decision Support Planning? p. 113, Chapter 7.

47. What Is ETL Software and How Is It Related to BI and Decision Support? p. 66, Chapter 4.

48. What Is Expected in Next-Generation Decision Support? p. 134, Chapter 8.

49. What Is Knowledge Management? p. 25, Chapter 2.

50. What Is Mobile Business Intelligence? p. 71, Chapter 4.

51. What Is Operational Business Intelligence? p. 22, Chapter 2.

52. What Is the Best Method for Building an Enterprise-Wide, Data-Driven Decision Support Application? p. 62, Chapter 4.

53. What Is the History of Computerized Decision Support? p. 7, Chapter 1.

54. What Is the Need for Decision Support? p. 2, Chapter 1.

55. What Is the Theory of Computerized Decision Support? p. 11, Chapter 1.

56. What Is Typical of Modern Decision Support? p. 14, Chapter 1.

57. What Questions Are Important for Evaluating a BI Data-Driven Decision Support Proposal? p. 55, Chapter 4.

58. What SQL Knowledge Do Managers Need for Decision Support Queries? p. 61, Chapter 4.

59. What Type of DSS is the System or Subsystem? p. 49, Chapter 3.

60. When Is Formative Rather than Summative Evaluation Used? p. 127, Chapter 8.

61. Who Uses Computerized Decision Support? p. 5, Chapter 1.

OTHER TITLES IN OUR INFORMATION SYSTEMS COLLECTION

Daniel J. Power, University of Northern Iowa and DSSResources.com, Collection Editor

- *Process Mapping and Management* by Sue Conger
- *The Art of Successful Information Systems Outsourcing* by David Gefen
- *Building Successful Information Systems: Five Best Practices to Ensure Organizational Effectiveness and Profitability* by Michael Savoie
- *Sales Technology: Making the Most of Your Investment* by Nikolaos Panagopoulos
- *Effective Sales Force Automation and Customer Relationship Management: A Focus on Selection and Implementation* by Raj Agnihotri
- *Supply Chain Risk Management: Tools for Analysis* by David Olson

---

Announcing the Business Expert Press Digital Library

Concise E-books Business Students Need for Classroom and Research

This book can also be purchased in an e-book collection by your library as
- a one-time purchase,
- that is owned forever,
- allows for simultaneous readers,
- has no restrictions on printing, and
- can be downloaded as PDFs from within the library community.

Our digital library collections are a great solution to beat the rising cost of textbooks. e-books can be loaded into their course management systems or onto student's e-book readers.

The **Business Expert Press** digital libraries are very affordable, with no obligation to buy in future years. For more information, please visit **www.businessexpertpress.com/librarians**. To set up a trial in the United States, please contact **Adam Chesler** at *adam.chesler@businessexpertpress .com* for all other regions, contact **Nicole Lee** at *nicole.lee@igroupnet.com*.

CPSIA information can be obtained at www.ICGtesting.com
Printed in the USA
BVOW03s2051171213

339143BV00005B/16/P